Sharing My Shoes

A Walk through the Journey of Forgiveness

Tammy Gaffney

Gazelle
PRESS

Mobile, Alabama

Gazelle Press
P.O. Box 191540 • Mobile, AL 36619
800-367-8203

Table of Contents

Technology

warren Buffect

Acknowledgments

I want to acknowledge my agent, Mr. Keith Carroll, because for three years he helped me through this journey, patiently waiting and encouraging me. He is truly a man of God, and I needed for him to join my path to help get my book out to you. He knows the Word and believes in the power and importance of forgiveness. Thanks, Mr. Carroll.

I thank my editors who worked tirelessly with me. They were patient and humble and didn't get offended when I kept questioning their editing. I just didn't want the "heart" of the message to get lost. I wanted to tell you everything and I couldn't. They knew how to put in just enough. Thank you both.

I would also like to thank my pastor and his wife, Kevin and Tanya James, at New Community Bible Fellowship, for being godly leaders who teach biblical sound doctrine, making disciples to have relationships with God. They also allowed me to teach the ministry of forgiveness at our church.

I thank my godly, loving husband, Magic, of twenty-two years. It is because of him besides my God that I know love and I am who I am today. I thank you for our partnership, commitment, patience, and belief in me and my dreams. I thank our daughters, Morgan and Miranda, and our son, Makale, for their love and patience and sacrifice while I was broken, sick, and pursuing my purpose. I'm thankful for you believing in me and allowing me to teach you how to not get trapped by anger and pain.

I thank my Granny, Mrs. Anderson, who will be 101 this year 2016. She has always believed in me and championed me to finish this book. Finally, I thank my parents, David and Mary. They love me so much, that even though this story has some tears, for the joy and healing it will bring the world, they unselfishly gave me permission and support to *Share My Shoes.*

Finally I thank all of my family and friends who prayed for me to finish this book. I thank all the people who trusted God with their hearts and allowed me to share this message. Now I thank you who will make this leap of faith and take this journey.

915

Cameo
    white

Benjamin moore

pucker Tom

poc
330

w/o —

Introduction

On November 17, 2015 I received a frantic, hysterical, indiscernible call. Someone was crying uncontrollably, but I could not understand who it was or what they were saying. After what seemed like hours passed while I tried to calm the person down, I finally said, "Please, I can't understand what you're saying. Who is this?" After a moment of silence the caller said, "I'm Karla; Momma is dead."

Karla is my niece but when she said "Momma," I didn't know if she was talking about her mother, who is also my sister Willow, or my own mother. My heart was racing because I didn't know if I was supposed to cry for my sister or my mother, but I had to hold it together to be strong for my niece.

My mother had raised Karla for most of her life because my sister had struggled with drug addiction for many years, and they had an estranged relationship. I'll be honest with you—my niece hated her mother. She only felt this way because she was deceived by the pain in her heart and the silence of her thoughts that tormented her. She thought my sister didn't love her.

However, she didn't understand that my sister carried a pain of her own that she tried to mask with drugs that made it appear as if she didn't love her family. Pain lies and holds everyone captive until the truth is able to enter. Neither of them had learned how to be set free from it instead of being held captive. I had never heard Karla refer to my sister as her mother or call her Mom. She only called her by her given name, so I was confused. I asked, "What Momma are you referring to?"

She said proudly, "my Momma Willow," and she hung up the phone. I burst into tears for my sister and at the fact that now when my sister was dead, her child finally called her "Mom." My heart was also hurting for my niece because I didn't want Karla to be tormented with unresolved issues of unforgiveness that would plague her with guilt. At the time I was unaware of the extraordinary blessing the two of them had shared shortly before my sister's death, which allowed Karla to utter the word "Momma."

This amazing story spurred me on to completing this book that I have been writing for twenty years. The book is birthed out of my own pain and life experiences, from teaching classes on forgiveness for over fifteen years, and out of diligently studying the Bible. God planted this seed in my heart at age nine to share the Gospel about how to love. When I discovered my purpose was to teach forgiveness, and I shared this ministry, I was surprised that I didn't see as many breakthroughs in people's lives as I had hoped for. I knew God's Word would deliver them from their past, but I had to find a way to convince them that forgiveness was the way. And then God revealed to me that unresolved pain is the barrier to people being able to receive the teaching about forgiveness.

At first I was using a traditional approach that hindered people. I call this the Pulpit Approach: Give a scripture; remind them that they are sinners; remind them that God forgave them; ignore their pain and anger toward God; and just expect them to forgive because God said to do it. I've discovered this approach makes people more angry and afraid to trust in the God who allowed their pain. God showed me a more effective way to teach forgiveness; however, it requires the one leading to be honest and transparent about how they arrived at a place of forgiveness.

I thought God took me into the classroom as the teacher, but I became the student. I had to learn to reach people's hearts and discover what they needed before they were ready to learn about forgiveness. At first I wasn't reaching them because I had wanted to just talk about forgiveness. I was very prepared with all the principles, definitions, and steps on how and why we are to forgive. However, the more I spoke about forgiveness, the more the group participants would get upset. I couldn't understand why people who signed up for a class about forgiveness were getting angry when they were asked to forgive. Let me share some more of my conversation with Karla to show you what I needed to learn in the classroom back then. It's the whole basis for this book.

I asked her, "When did you start calling Willow, Momma?" She said, "Two months ago." Prior to the death of my sister, the two of them were together! She said, "Just out of nowhere God brought the two of us together." Mind you, she had been angry with God and refused to believe in Him for twenty years until just two months earlier!

Karla explained to me that her momma called and asked her, "Why do you hate me?" She wanted to know what she had done to her daughter. Karla said, "I just let her have it. I didn't hold back my pain anymore. I told her everything I was carrying in my heart, including my anger over her addiction and my feeling like I was never accepted. I asked her why did I have to live with Grandma, but her other children stayed with her?" Karla always felt like her older siblings were closer to Willow because they shared in her struggles and as a result, Karla thought Willow loved them more.

Karla said she let it all out until there was nothing left to say. Then suddenly she felt a cleansing. A burden lifted from her and she was free! She said, "Auntie, when I got that pain out of my soul, I could see my momma again and love began to enter my heart." She said she felt born again—like a new woman. This is the central message of this book: helping you get free from your pain first and then walking you through the journey of forgiveness.

As she told me her story, tears streamed down my face. My heart rejoiced. I could hardly believe what she was saying. As we talked, we both would chime in using the same words describing how she feels now and we'd start laughing. I told her, "You couldn't even believe in God or trust Him until you confessed your pain. Before, you were too angry to let Him in."

She replied, "That's right, Auntie, but how did you know?" I told her, "I've written a book about it, which shows people how to experience this kind of healing. I sent it to my agent already, but what you have shared with me is the final confirmation that it's time for this journey to begin." I asked her if I could use her story and she said, "If your book will give people what I experienced with my momma in these last two months, then yes—the world will be blessed."

Karla says that after her own pain ended, she saw Willow as a person with wounds and brokenness of her own—not just as her mother. When she asked her mom why she did drugs, her mom shared the pain of how she had been molested as a child but had never been able to tell anyone. She had just buried that anger, which turned into bitterness that took her hostage, robbing her of being a sister, a daughter, and a mother. It wasn't just her past but being consumed (full of) pain and anger that cut her dreams short.

Willow and Karla talked for hours, cried, and then talked and cried some more. Karla said she and her mom exchanged their pain, meaning they allowed each other the freedom and safety to bare their soul. After that they both were free: there was no more anger, guilt, debt, pain, tears, or any place to bring up the past again.

They were finally ready to live in the present, and their mutual love and forgiveness would keep them there. What each of them did, in a metaphorical sense, was to share their shoes (their story) with each other through their journey of pain. That was the first step in their journey of deliverance—facing the pain of the past.

We have to stop telling people to forgive before we have allowed them to get rid of their pain. They have to start with their pain before they can forgive. Giving up their pain unlocks the love in their hearts, which brings forgiveness. This summarizes what *Sharing My Shoes* is all about.

Karla shared with me that, from that point on, every weekend she came up to see her mother. They also talked on the phone. She said that the two months of love they shared erased the previous twenty-four years of anger, pain, bitterness, and suffering. Until two months earlier, Karla couldn't remember anything good about her past. She had been seeing a psychologist for four years, trying to remember something good. But now in one moment, by confessing her pain, getting free, walking in love, and choosing to forgive, it happened.

Up until then, she was not able to fall asleep very easily; and when she did, she needed a light or TV on, in addition to medication. Since then she hasn't had to take medication or sleep with the lights on. Karla says now when she thinks of her mother it is like a beautiful breeze on a summer day—a refreshing feeling. After she gave her pain up, Karla didn't have to think or talk about it again. Now Karla's free and my sister died knowing she had reconciled with her children and helped them not carry the burden of pain and anger any longer.

That day when I received the call from Karla, we both were crying for the same reason: the death of Willow—the passing of a mother and sister. Karla said having loved her momma for two months was worth not having her in her life for twenty-four years. This speaks of the power and value of love!

We buried my beautiful, strong sister Willow on November 22, 2015. She left behind seven wonderful children. We celebrated her life that she had re-dedicated to the Lord on May 31, 2015. She had been reconciled with her pain, her mistakes, and her family all because she finally confessed her pain and surrendered through love and forgiveness.

Willow was getting ready to go back to school to become a drug counselor, since she had fought her addiction and remained clean for several years. She hasn't gotten to share her story the way she thought she would, but everyone who reads this book, takes this journey, and gets delivered through love and forgiveness, can have their yesterdays transformed like my Willow and Karla did. To help you in your journey, I will share my life, my journey, "My Shoes," to help you learn how to live a life free, blessed, and living in love, that's how you get on the path of forgiveness.

My Own Story

I was rejected by my biological father, molested by my stepfather, and I felt betrayed by my mother because she didn't believe me at first. She thought I was just being a rebellious teenager, trying to get rid of authority in my life. My stepfather stayed in our home, pretending to be the innocent one, and I left to live with my grandparents. I got involved with a religious organization that took the place of God in my life, leaving me at the brink of wanting to take my own life. I was almost destroyed. I dedicated my life to them and married one of their ministers; he too abused me more than I could ever imagine. I later discovered that a person I loved like a sister was a part of a conspiracy that led to my husband becoming jealous, his beating me, and filing for divorce. After many years of living in anger, pain, and finding my way back to God, He put the ministry of forgiveness in my heart and now He wants me to share this journey of deliverance from my past life—a story of God's unfathomable love and wonderful healing.

The love I now share with my parents is so great and the place where we have come from is so different, that I had to share the journey. Both my parents are alive and know that I'm writing this book. They are aware how broken I was because of pain and anger, and what forgiveness and love did for our family so they gave me their permission to share this with you. It will be a little bumpy at times (even for you, Mom and Dad, to read this because, although you know my story, I never shared all of my pain). I never really knew it myself until God allowed me to take this journey.

Today, people are being asked to forgive the past, but they don't even know what's really hurting their heart. This journey—this book—will help you find out "What Really Has Bound Your Heart," which is the title of one of the chapters. You can't forgive what you have not confessed or are unaware is hurting you. You can't even heal until you confess your pain and get it out. Sometimes you need time to regurgitate the past to have a sense of why you keep reliving the same mistakes over and over again. The answers from the past will help free you from living a life that God has not destined for you. It will help you understand why you are sabotaging yourself.

I couldn't write about this journey standing "behind the pulpit." When I say pulpit, I'm not disrespecting the Church or God's people or His Word because my book is all about God. I'm just saying there is nothing cute about pain or unforgiveness, and I had to write the truth about how to get darkness out of our hearts and forgive. This is what I learned when I tried to first teach in the classroom. I couldn't just use the scriptures to explain forgiveness, I had to show you my life and share My Shoes. I want to teach you how to become free from your pain, learn how to love yourself and love those who afflicted you, trust in God, and find forgiveness.

It has taken me a long time to write this book because now I realize my life had to come full circle in order to share these things with you. (Willow, that includes waiting awhile to allow a little of your story to come through too. Nothing we do is wasted, so He did allow you to tell your story, Sis; it was just through me. Love you.)

Before we get started, I want to share with you how God revealed to me that the place to start with hurting people wasn't in forgiveness. I had to go where they were and meet them there. This is the reason for the journey. In the classroom, I saw firsthand that although a hurting person may be in the present physically, everything else about them was still in the past—the heart and soul. It was what I learned from teaching forgiveness in the classroom that showed me how to share this truth.

God taught me through the book of Job the importance of allowing others to deal with their pain before we can give advice. Job says, "Do you think your words are convincing when you disregard my cry of desperation?" (6:26 NLT) Likewise when religious leaders or friends refuse to hear your cry and see your pain, they allow your anger to grow and it becomes an obstacle that blocks your heart from receiving counsel from God. Preventing or discouraging people from confessing or sharing their pain is the barrier that has prevented some from experiencing forgiveness in their life. When we ignore their cries, we can't preach the message that will penetrate their heart.

This book will show you not only how to have your pain heard but also the purpose and the power in it, and how forgiveness will bless you. I understand it because of where I have come from and want to bring you a new perspective on forgiveness. Come join me on this journey.

~ 1 ~
The Reason for the Journey

I always knew that I wanted to help God's people. I had a heart to reach out to hurting people even as a child because I was extra sensitive to people who suffered in any way. I had experienced pain in my life, and through forgiveness, grace, mercy, and God's love, I made it through. I wanted to share the ministry of forgiveness with others. People recognized a gift of wisdom in me to give godly advice, and many times I was asked to counsel people, couples, and families to work through their relationship difficulties with forgiveness.

After the success I saw in the restoration work of forgiveness in people's lives, I wanted to write a book to share on a larger scale the same insights God was giving me. I gathered all my study lessons and wrote a manuscript and submitted it to publishers about fifteen years ago. I received good feedback from editors and agents, but no one would represent me. I became discouraged because of one rejection after another so I thought maybe a book wasn't the right direction on which to focus my teaching on forgiveness.

I set the forgiveness book aside for the time being. However, I was still being asked to intervene to help people in their relationships, and I saw that what I did was effective. God put a yearning in my spirit again to lead His people into forgiveness, but I didn't know how this was going to manifest itself. In the meantime, while I was waiting for a door to open, God was speaking to me in my dreams. I would wake up with a wealth of insight about forgiveness that I couldn't explain or understand—amazing revelations about the power of forgiveness and how to forgive.

All of a sudden, without my talking with anyone, my pastor asked me what I was passionate about. One thing led to another and I was asked if I would start teaching classes on forgiveness. I was so excited! I didn't care whether I had written a book or not; I just didn't want to waste all that God had given me and not help His people. I wanted to show people that forgiveness really does work. I knew it did, because not only did I teach it to people, it had saved my life. Had I not learned how to forgive, I would not be here today. I believed in forgiveness because I lived it.

The day came when the classes in forgiveness began. I was so happy. I knew the breakthroughs the women would experience if they would receive the teaching and apply it to their lives. I had prepared well. I am a diligent studier of the Bible. I had all my information, handouts, steps, principles, takeaways, and application exercises ready. If they wanted to learn how to forgive, they would absolutely get that from my class. However, forgiveness can't be reached through mere head knowledge; it is reached only through the heart.

The first week in a new group is always exciting for everyone. We introduced ourselves just to feel comfortable with one another. I told the class I was going to be real and transparent. I told them we were going to deal with forgiveness, even the difficult parts. I told them they could express themselves freely without condemnation and assured them this would be an environment in which they could ask any question they had on their heart. They were given the syllabus so they knew that we were going to tackle some heavy topics surrounding forgiveness. Nevertheless, they left with smiles on their faces, hope in their eyes, and an attitude of readiness to conquer their past and forgive. This was a dream come true!

To my surprise all the members returned to the next class and some brought friends and family. My classes were often so full we had to add another room to accommodate everyone. I couldn't believe all these people were ready to surrender and forgive, but what happened next baffled me.

The first lesson I taught was taken from John 5. It's the story of a man who suffered with an infirmity for over thirty years. Jesus asked him if he wanted to be healed. Using this story as a starting point, I hoped to discuss the reasons why we delay our healing by focusing on our past. I wanted to discuss the importance of making the decision to be healed and taking our eyes off our pain.

I thought this would empower the women, but as I looked around in the room, the hope I had seen in their eyes began to dissipate. Anger arose in its place and was trying to snuff out their optimism. I saw their pain as eyes began to fill with tears. I hadn't even mentioned the word "forgive" when suddenly there was a shift in the atmosphere—a darkness, sadness, and air of mistrust permeated the room. Instead of being the likeable teacher who was going to help, I somehow had become a part of their problem.

An uncomfortable quiet filled the room and someone

blurted out, "Why should I forgive someone who hurt me? How will forgiving bless me? The people who hurt me are fine, living their life; they don't need my forgiveness." Others chimed in saying they were hurting and unable to trust anyone. Some even accused God, asking how could a loving God allow them to be hurt and do nothing. I could tell they were sharing their hearts without reservation in a way they probably had not done in a long time. Because some of them were thinking about their pain, they were now questioning the rationality of forgiveness.

At the end of the session, all our hearts were heavy. This was a class about forgiveness but without even using the word, I saw pain and anger. I thought the only lesson in the story from John 5 was that if you want to be healed, you must stop making excuses and begin to obey what God says—in this case, forgive. However, as I looked closer and saw the tears streaming, I realized that there is a place to deal with the pain of the past before you can obey and get healed. This man had to first talk about his past even though Christ stood before him with all power to heal him. Pain was still on his mind, and it couldn't be ignored. I learned I would need to open the door for them to address their pain before they could continue their journey toward forgiveness

Most of the women returned to complete the classes. However it was a struggle to teach. Weeks passed and I had not been able to get into the meat of my lessons. Every time I tried to talk about forgiveness, the women just wanted to share more of their pain. I thought they were trying to convince me how terrible their life was and that some things couldn't be forgiven. Without fail, whenever I told them that despite their pain they still had to forgive, they would ask,

"Who are you? Why should we listen to you?" That was followed by, "You have not walked in our shoes."

Week after week they kept asking me, "Who are you?" I didn't understand the question or the point. But the question was deeper than they or I realized. Instead of asking God what they meant when they asked the question, I kept thinking if they would just study the materials they would get their breakthrough. However, the breakthrough they were looking for wasn't going to be found in paper handouts.

I didn't realize they had never been loosed from their pain. I wanted them to understand forgiveness, but God showed me I was trying to teach from the head and not the heart. They needed to get free first in their heart, and then they could choose to make the decision to forgive.

It took me awhile to get it, but I finally realized there has to be a place to deal with the past in teaching forgiveness. Once I saw this, I stopped resisting their need to talk out their pain. Pain was always present, but I needed to acknowledge it before I could get the women's attention.

As the class ended, I left them with a folder full of handouts and prayed they would read them and get delivered. Thank God for His grace and love because they didn't need me to get delivered. The women who wanted deliverance received it. For years afterward, I felt I had fallen short with that first class. I thought I had been called to lead the class as the teacher, but God showed me I had a lot to learn myself. I finally understood what those women needed to hear when they asked, "Who are you?" and discovered the connection they needed from me to teach them how to forgive.

Thankfully, we saw some breakthroughs with those women. There were enough positive testimonies that I was asked to teach the same subject the following year. I was excited and anxious as I prepared for the next class. This time I made a place for the women to share their stories. I assured them nothing would be repeated outside that room, and that's the way it has been for fifteen years. I never know what to expect when they open up.

As before, the first week of introductions and sharing was great. The real test for the success of the class was going to be weeks two and three. In the second week I allowed them to share their pain, and it happened again. The women didn't want to do anything else but talk about their pain. And like before, many of the women became very emotional.

As this was happening, I thought to myself, *Most of these women are Christians, some are leaders themselves, and yet they are pushing back against forgiveness.* I wondered how I was going to teach when all they wanted to do was cry. When I tried to regain control over the class and redirect the focus to forgiveness, it happened again: "Who are you to tell me to forgive? You never walked in my shoes. You don't know what I went through. If you understood, you wouldn't be telling me to forgive. Why did God allow all this pain in my life? He could have stopped it."

I was glad to know what was bothering them, but I still didn't understand why they kept asking, "Who are you?" What did I have to do with them forgiving someone else? Why were they coming to a class about forgiveness if I had to convince them that they needed to forgive? I couldn't understand why this was happening again. I knew this wasn't about any pride. I really wanted to help them. Something was missing and I had to find the connection between them sharing their stories and me knowing when it was time to teach about forgiveness. I had finally realized that forgiveness wasn't the place to begin, but I had to find out where to start.

I came to understand what they meant when they asked who I was—they wanted to know if I was just another instructor who was going to supply them with information, because no matter how biblically sound it was, they needed more than that. They had been in a dry, barren place for too long and were tired of pretending everything was okay. The pain was eating them alive, and they couldn't hold it in any longer. When it finally came out, there were no apologies for the anger.

They wanted to know if the person standing in front of them knew where they were coming from and cared about them. They didn't want to waste my time or theirs. They had already wasted many of their years. I started to pay attention to something they said repeatedly when I told them to forgive. They said I hadn't walked in their shoes.

After the third week I asked God, "What do I have to do with their forgiving and their shoes? I'm not You. Help me, Father, I want to help Your people and not bring them more harm." Then God, in His love and wisdom, opened my eyes to see what was going on. He said, "Everything!"

I'm thinking, *Okay, what does He mean by "everything"?* This was when the real revelation came, and it has changed my approach to teaching forgiveness forever. God said in my spirit, "You have everything to do with their ability to forgive! They need to know what it took for you to forgive. Show them." As I thought about it, I started to realize their focus was all about their pain and all that had been done to them. Many of them have never had a chance to process it. No one ever checked their heart to see if they were okay. No one has ever allowed them to tell their whole story.

Everyone has told them to move on, but they can't move on because the past is a part of them just as much as their present. They do not know how to get free. This has allowed anger to continue to grow and become a stronghold in their life. Some people don't know they're not free from their past. But others can see it manifested in depression, divorce, and acceptance of abuse, alcoholism, drug addiction, sexual promiscuity, or a lack of self-esteem.

This stronghold of anger affects their health too, leading them to have high blood pressure, strokes, cancer, and much more. Anger is an internal poison that is a self-radical inside their own body to harm them. God said to me, "My people are suffering because no one will show them how to cry. They do want to forgive, but you and so many others are hindering them."

I thought, *How, when all I want to do is help them and teach them about forgiving?* The Lord helped me understand something. He said to me, "They do not want to listen to you because you don't see them. Meet them where they are—in their pain—and then you will have their attention."

A Lesson From Job

The Lord reminded me about the account of Job and all that he suffered: the tragedy of losing his children and his wealth, his wife telling him to curse his God, the debilitating sickness in his body, and his friends judging his motives when he tried to share his pain and not just retell events. He needed to share what pain was doing to him in his heart—it was tormenting him. He began saying things like he should have died at birth, cursed be his mother's womb for letting him live, no light should appear on his birthday and that the day should be taken off the calendar (Job 3:1-23 NLT). He even begged God to crush and kill him (Job 6:8 NLT). His pain took him to a dark place. Pain will cause your thinking to become twisted about who you were created to be. It will skew your perception of God and the world.

Instead of Job's companions seeing his pain and allowing him to express that the resultant darkness was invading his soul, they judged him. However, to help him get over his pain and questioning God for all that he was encountering, they tried to give him lots of advice. Because they wouldn't listen to him, Job said, "Do you think your words are convincing when you disregard my cry of desperation?" (Job 6:26 NLT). This is so powerful. I finally got it. The women in my class were desperate and hurting, but because I wasn't listening, their anger exploded. I wanted to give them sound advice, but it wasn't given at the proper time.

I thought I was doing them a favor by allowing them a little time to share their pain. I had it all wrong. I used to start teaching by talking about forgiveness, but I learned from those women and God that until we deal with the pain, we will never get started toward wholeness. They were entrusting not only their pain to me but they trusted me with their hearts, which was something many of them had kept hidden and tucked away for a long time.

Now I was beginning to understand. The women didn't want to listen to me because I wasn't seeing or listening to them. They needed for me to meet them where they were in their pain.

God took it one step further. He said, "When they ask, 'Who are you?' it's not about your credentials to teach—it's about your ability to lead. They want to know if you've been where the pain has taken them. Have you been in the place where you were tempted to curse Me?" Before, I could answer, He said, "Yes, you have been there too. Stop acting religious. Stop acting like you have always walked in My love, trusted Me, and never questioned Me. Stop acting like pain never twisted you. Get off your high horse.... Get real and share your story. I didn't send you into the wilderness to learn pain, love, and forgiveness for you to hide behind sermons. I sent you into the wilderness so that when you came out, I could use you. You have what these women want and need.

"I sent you into the classroom the first time to see what they wanted; now you're doing the same thing you did then. If you don't do what I sent you here to do, you will never write the book I put in your heart at [age] nine." A shift had occurred in my spirit as God was speaking to me. He was serious, and He was letting me know this was bigger than I realized. So I asked, "What do you want me to do?" He answered with a whisper so faint I almost wanted to dismiss it. He said, "Share your story."

God was telling me to stop trying to prove that I was capable of teaching. The women didn't want to be shown where a verse was in the Bible. They were needing to know where I had been and how had the Bible helped me. They wanted to be taught by someone who had walked in their shoes and had come out victorious on the other side.

God's instruction to me continued, "They need someone to show them unconditional love. Their breakthrough will come as they rediscover My love—embrace it, believe it, and walk in it. This will equip them to trust Me so they will be able to obey My Word and walk in forgiveness. I need someone who will show them what that looks like, not just give them words or a book to read. They can do that on their own. Share out of your own pain so that you will gain their trust, and I can reach their heart. Forgiveness is a heart matter, and everyone, including you, keeps trying to reach broken hearts through the head. Would you pour water into a broken vessel? No, you would repair it first. Take them through your journey so they can see how I healed your pain, and then they will be able to learn from your story. Share your shoes!"

To be honest, I didn't want to share my story with the class. I thought if I could just talk about forgiveness, they would see how blessed I was today and want to join me. I also didn't want to expose the hurt I had experienced with my family. I didn't want to hurt them or give people the wrong impression of them. However, we are all in a wonderful place now, and God said I needed to share my story. So humbly I submitted to Him and went back into the classroom.

To be honest, I had forgotten about the pain in my life. I've had to deal with the hurts and offenses of every day, but I do not allow things to become a stronghold over my heart. I had gotten over the pain that had almost destroyed me, the pain that almost caused me to commit suicide, the same pain that made me stop talking to God for three years. It was in the past and I never wanted to look back. However, God made me remember the journey it took to forgive.

God wants me to tell you I understand why you are afraid to forgive people who've hurt you—why you can't see any good in the people who made you a victim of your past. I understand the anger that rises in your heart every time when you think about the past and you are told to give grace, mercy, and love to people who robbed you of the very things you are being asked to give. I understand the big question, which you've buried very deep, but in the back of your mind it still lingers: "Why, God?" I understand why you have not shared your true heart because you don't want to be judged or misunderstood, just like Job who was blameless. I understand because I've been there myself!

Some need to be shown how to walk the journey because they got lost in the wilderness when they took their eyes off God and placed it on their pain. As time passes, they become more and more disconnected. The voice of light, truth, and love becomes snuffed out by the pain, darkness, and isolation with which they are surrounded. They can't see God any more, or they have forgotten what He looks like.

So I asked God, "Where do I start?" God said, "Start with where you were when you stopped talking to Me for three years, and what led up to that. Really share your feelings. Walk them through their pain and bring them to Me."

When the next week came, I began the class by sharing my story. I confessed, "I was mad at God. In fact I was so mad at Him that I didn't talk to Him for three years. I thought my life was better off without God and that He hated me." They couldn't believe it. Not Ms. Tammy, who drips love out of her mouth all the time about God. How could I ever be in a place where I was mad at Him and didn't talk with Him? They were surprised and relieved that I too had questioned His love to the point of thinking He hated me. At that point, I made a connection with the women again.

Oh, it was like being in a juicy movie to them. I had the women's attention from that point on. They wanted to hear me tell them what changed. How did I lay my anger down and trust God again? That's what forgiveness is about. It doesn't start with getting over being mad with man (that is the forgiveness we teach in the classroom). It really begins with becoming reconciled back with God. This is what you will get in this journey.

I told them what the pain had done to me—how it twisted my perception of myself, God, and my purpose in life. I once heard TD Jakes say, "Empathy is the capacity to understand from within where another person has been. It is the ability to understand what another person has experienced within the reference of their frame of mind. It is the ability to place oneself into another person's shoes." This was exactly what the women in those classes wanted: empathy. Sharing my shoes was proof.

A Thirty-Year Process

It has taken me over thirty years to write this book. Everything written is authentic. I will take you with me on my journey through my pain and see with me as I discovered what it really took to get to a place of trusting God, loving, and forgiving again. I invite you to come into my life to see my pain and how it affected me and to learn how to surrender your pain before God. I offer my life's story because God wanted you to have more than paper to read so I give you my flesh on forgiveness.

Unforgiveness is preventing God's people from having kingdom power in their lives, homes, and churches. If I can help even one person on this journey then it was worth it. We have to wake up to this weapon the enemy is using against us. Some of you haven't been able to hear the counsel about forgiveness because of your pain, so in this journey I will share with you how to reconcile with it so you can move on, obey God, and walk in the purpose He has destined for your life.

The second part of this book will show you how to forgive by applying God's Word to your life. I show you what I did instead of telling you what to do. I invite you to come along on this journey and learn how to conquer your pain so you can walk in forgiveness and never have to be a prisoner of your past again.

I began writing this book after I was diagnosed with a brain aneurysm. I've had three brain surgeries and suffer with chronic, debilitating headaches. However, now I can be trusted to not turn against God or think He has turned His back on me when I am in the midst of my storms.

I love the Lord and He loves me, and I want to share with you how to never allow pain to be a greater voice than God's ever again. Pain is what blocks or hardens the heart from wanting to forgive. Pain un-acknowledged is the soil for anger to grow in, and anger is the fertilizer for unforgiveness—all three go hand-in-hand. However, we can't continue to talk about anger and forgiveness and ignore pain; that is the error that has held so many people captive to their past.

I just bought a new crockpot and was looking at recipes for beans. One recipe cautioned the cook to be sure that the beans were fully cooked before adding sugar because it will prevent the beans from getting soft and the recipe will not turn out right. In other words, the sugar will make the beans hard if you add it before the right time.

How interesting it is that something which is sweet and can make something taste good, could also, if added at the wrong time, make that same thing hard and distasteful. So I

14

compared this concept with forgiveness. Forgiveness is something good; I will even liken it to sugar. When it is added at the right time, it brings a change, a softening, and sweetness within a person's heart (crockpot). People who give forgiveness (sugar) cause others to want to be around (taste) them because when they feel good about themselves, they make others feel good too.

On the other hand, if you try to add forgiveness to the recipe (a person's broken heart) before they are ready, before they have had time to deal with their pain, identified what they are angry about, and have had their cry with God about those "why" questions they are still carrying around, it won't work. Some of the questions they have to let go, but some have to be addressed, confessed, and confronted before people will be able to move on. If you try to pour the sugar (forgiveness) on them before they are ready, you might harden their hearts even further.

If you want a book that will be more than someone telling you to forgive while never showing you what that even looks like or why it really matters, then read on. I'll also share what to do with your pain while you're waiting for that miracle called forgiveness to work in and bless your life. I'll show you how God loved you despite allowing your pain. I will take you through my own process of pain and how God healed me. The journey begins with me teaching in the classroom, moving at times between my past and present as I navigated through my life and discovered what it really took to forgive. I adapted the classroom experience and opened it for you to come along and make it your own. This is a journey filled with revelations to unlock the mysteries behind what has kept you bound and what God revealed to me to set us free.

~ 2 ~

Sharing My Shoes

It was so quiet you could hear a pin drop. I didn't know I was going to be so transparent that day in the classroom while sharing that I had been angry with God. I just blurted it out. I let them see my anger and pain. I had once had issues with God too. This was what they wanted to hear. They needed to know I had been where they had been. Pain had once driven a wedge between me and God too.

Like a flood God brought it all back. It was as though I were living in the past all over again. I was a little girl who fell in love with God at age nine and cherished our relationship. We had history. Then I had dissociated myself with Him—my Father, God, and Friend. That was one of the darkest times in my life. Now I remember why I never wanted to think about that time again and why it was so hard to connect with the women in the class. Our worlds were so far apart. Once I had gotten out of that place, I never wanted to look back, and I was trying to prevent others from going back too. However, the truth is you can't run, hide, or deny your past. You have to confront it in truth and God's love. I finally did receive the victory over my past, and I needed to go back in time to show the class how to get out.

My story begins when I had stopped talking to God for

trust him as a virtuous man. However, I would soon find out virtue and my husband didn't exist together except for when he put on a pretense at our place of worship.

I still believed in myself and believed that God loved me. Satan tried to rob me of my identity as a young girl, but it hadn't worked. Since he was unable to destroy me back then, now he was trying to use my husband to fulfill his plan. However, as long as I believed in God's love, the enemy couldn't defeat me. It didn't matter that my husband was trying to hurt me; I was more than a conqueror.

Eventually, Stanley's verbal abuse turned physical. He'd break up the furniture and punch holes in the wall. He wouldn't let me use the phone, drive the car without him, or see my family. And he did hit me. I was devastated. How could this happen? How did I open the door for Stanley to enter my heart?

I wasn't a person to allow abuse in my life. I was a fighter. It wasn't because of love I tried to make it work. It was because I didn't want to look like a failure or be blamed for another relationship in my life not working like I felt as a child. I was afraid of being judged. But ultimately I didn't want to give up my faith. My religion controlled my beliefs, and I thought they were the only way to get to God.

I remember when we were engaged, one of the church elders referred to Stanley as the "cream of the crop." I was told to feel honored to have been chosen by him. I didn't know if anyone would believe me if I told them what their perfect Stanley was doing. I couldn't share this with my family because I didn't associate with them a lot because of my faith and because I was ashamed.

Stanley's personality was so volatile. Once we were driving to work together on the freeway. He knew I was afraid to drive on the freeway because I had been in a recent accident. To harass me, he told me to switch places with him so I could drive. Mind you, he was in the driver's seat. I said no and he then tried to jump onto my lap. At that point, I tried to jump into the backseat. (Yes, we were going 55 mph at the time!) As I jumped into the back seat, he bit my leg. I later arrived at work, limping, with blood oozing through my pants, and made up a story like most abused women do.

After many irrational incidents like this, I decided to go to the Elders at our worship center. I needed help and I had to humble myself and confess my pain. They arranged for a meeting for my husband and I to get counsel. I hadn't given up on the marriage yet. I had hoped we could get on the right track. To my surprise the session really became a "how to be a better wife" session. Stanley was so good at portraying me as a very difficult, aggressive person who wore him down. He lost his anger mildly in an outburst of frustration because of his wife and told them he was afraid of me. Before the meeting was over, they were comforting him. I got so upset. I couldn't believe what was transpiring in front of me—they were consoling Stanley! I lost it.

I didn't have any tears left by that time—all they saw was my anger. People judge you when they see your anger; they don't want to acknowledge the pain that causes it. So after that there was no help for me there. In seeing my anger they believed his whole story. It didn't matter about the visible bruises or my tears.

Now I remember why I hadn't wanted to revisit this place. It had been twenty-four years since I was there mentally, emotionally, and spiritually. I'm free now but I had to remember the dreadful, lonely place where I once had lived. I had to go back into my past to show hurting people how forgiveness works. It was here where I had started losing my faith.

I remember how frustrating it felt being judged by people who failed to see my pain. How could I be there crying my heart out, even having physical scars, and they ignore it? They just wanted to give me advice. They had infuriated me. God had me look back into my journey because I needed to remember how it felt to be in pain and be ignored by people who thought they had the answers but would not care about your story. The healing begins in the story. My husband left that meeting feeling better because they listened to his pain (even if it was a lie). I just wanted the same attention and concern from them.

After remembering all this, I finally started to understand the frustration of the class who, when sharing their pain, felt judged before they finished their story. That's what happened to me, and now I could see that's what I had done to them. I thought they wanted to make excuses and didn't want to forgive. I just saw their anger like the elders saw mine—they didn't want to also acknowledge my pain. They just wanted me to move on. However, I couldn't move on because they never addressed the situation—the pain—they just wanted to give counsel about the anger. I needed to bottle that experience and take it back into the classroom with me.

My heart was so heavy back then. I was in a room with several elders and my husband. These were the people who were supposed to protect, teach, and lead me. I was so broken. It's easy to forget how you feel in the wilderness when you are free today. Who wants to remember oneself as a hopeless, helpless, vulnerable person? However, this is what I had to do to prove I had walked in their shoes.

I can hardly believe as I look back that this was me. I love God today with all my heart, but in that moment I remembered how alienated I was from Him. I wasn't just angry; I didn't want anything to do with Him. I was tired of Him not protecting me. My soul was weary. I had held on to trusting Him and He kept letting me down. I wondered. *Why God? I loved you as a little girl. I didn't stop loving you when I was molested and now you allowed a false witness to abuse my love too. Why wouldn't you at least allow the elders to see the bruises on me and that I was telling the truth? Why do I have to always carry the burdens of the sins of people done against me and keep walking in faith? When was faith going to work for me?*

When I first started teaching, I didn't understand that the ladies needed the opportunity to speak honestly before their Father. I didn't need to defend God. I needed to allow them to get in His presence. The key to their breakthrough would be drawing near to God with their hearts.

I'm taking time to share the way I was feeling in the wilderness because I want you to know how to begin your journey. At this moment you may feel like the situation in front of you is what is causing your pain; but as you begin this journey, you'll discover there are things in your past you never dealt with that are the root to your pain. God allowed me to revisit my past so I could help you learn how to unlock the truth in it that is robbing you of your blessings today.

When I opened up to the women, initially I confessed I was angry with God because I was getting a divorce. However, as I began to share what was at the root of my pain, I saw that it was more than just me getting a divorce. It's important to discover what is feeding your pain. Journaling will help you discover the answers. Sometimes you can't get delivered because what you're complaining about isn't the real problem. So there is no resolution. The past will keep returning to your mind, trying to trap you until you attack it at the root.

Looking back, I remembered how there was a short period when I stopped participating in my religion before I married Stanley. I was dating someone else named Charles at the time who didn't share the same religious faith. Although I had stopped attending the meetings, I still continued to believe only in their teachings. They were so strict, however, I needed to make sure if I wanted to commit my life to them. Charles and I had a very special relationship. He was good to me and we loved each other, but he always said he would never accept my religion. Because I believed in my heart I had found the true religion and decided I didn't want to be affiliated with any other one, I broke my relationship off with him. I felt like I had to make a choice, and I chose God and let Charles go. I thought God would bless me with extra favor because I made a sacrifice for Him. This was why I was so mad at God.

Those of you who feel disappointed in how your life has turned out or who are angry at God need to get it all out now so that you can finally begin to heal. (Or you can just wait until reading about the end of the journey to see how God mended my heart back together before you open up yours.) Just as I felt like I had given up everything, even love, but could not see what He had given me, I want you to be real with God too. Ask Him to reveal what really has you broken.

I returned back to the organization, and Stanley and I

had married six months later. (They didn't encourage long courtships to prevent sexual immorality.) I thought he would love me like God did. Or really I thought God would ensure that he'd love me because I had given up my love of Charles for my faith. Charles never abused me and he had more faith than Stanley. Now I realize external works don't necessarily mean you are who you say you are. Had I been aware, I could have protected myself; but to be honest, it might not have mattered. We always think about what we could have done differently when we see things in hindsight.

I was blind. I had never doubted for one moment that Stanley was a godly man who would show me unconditional love. And I was mad at God for letting me give up Charles who really loved me. I felt like God had let me down.

Being broken wasn't what I had bargained for—not that any of us would choose to be divorced, depressed, and hopeless. However, when I accepted God into my life, I had such high expectations. No one prepared me for the suffering. No one told me that God still loved me even when He allowed pain and that He would bring good out of it (Rom. 8:28).

These may not be your issues. Maybe you never were mad at God; maybe it was something entirely different. Nevertheless, you need to start looking into your past to see why you have arrived at the place where you are today. Before you quickly say nothing is wrong, just think about some of these questions: What's making your heart sad? Why are you easily offended? Why does everything have to be your way? Why don't your relationships last? Why haven't you spoken to your mother, father, sister, brother, or children in years? Why don't you go to church but you believe in God? Why do you push people out of your life at any hint of conflict? Why do you fall in love as quickly as you fall out of it? Your past holds the answers.

I wasn't mad because of the things that happened to me. I was mad at God because I felt He hadn't protected me from the resulting pain and disappointment. I had given my life to Him when I was nine and He was the center of my world. I guess I thought I was someone special and was above being hurt and let down. I didn't realize that He uses pain to refine us not because He is against us. The women in my class needed to realize this too in order to get past their pain and anger and fall in love with Him all over again.

I remember, as a child, writing letters to people in the phone book, telling them how much God loved them. I would visit the widowed women in my neighborhood, listening to their stories and crying with them. As a little girl I knew I was destined to walk with women in their pain, however I never thought I would have to experience it myself. I thought I could just be sympathetic and understand their journey. I later learned that some connections only come when two people share a common path.

I'll never forget how I felt seeing their frowns turn into smiles. It didn't take much—just a little kindness mixed with God's truth. Why wasn't it that simple in the classroom? Was it because those women had already learned how to deal with their pain? I needed to learn what the women knew that brought them to the point in life where, despite being old or alone, simply being reminded of God's love was enough to put their world back in order.

My family thought I was strange because all I ever wanted to talk about was God. The truth is, nothing ever satisfied me as much back then, or today, as God does. That's another reason why I was so angry with Him. I had made Him my all in all, and this was the thanks I got—being constantly abused. I didn't understand His plans for me. When God didn't do the things I thought He should do for me, I stopped trusting Him. Actually, I allowed my pain to change my perception toward God, and in some ways He was no longer God to me. This is very difficult to admit, but why else would we allow pain to separate us from God?

Breaking Point

When I was divorcing Stanley and began blaming God, I stopped talking with Him. I was at my breaking point. I didn't know what to do. I was disappointed with life and became stuck. I turned my back on God and refused to go near Him. I began to suffer and continued to suffer until I was willing, or someone was willing, to take me to Jesus again. This is what the women were experiencing when I met them in class. Some had turned their backs on God. Some were not ready to trust Him with their hearts. Some were ready to unload their pain, and they were not going to let me or anything stop them from bringing their hearts to Him.

Although I had been in a loveless and abusive marriage, I was told by the elders I couldn't divorce so I tried to make it work. Stanley did everything to sabotage our marriage and make me feel dirty, unworthy, and uncomfortable with my beauty and sexuality. I hated having sex. He made what was supposed to be a beautiful part of marriage, lovemaking, something demeaning. I felt empty and alone. I came to the place where if I had to stay with him, I wanted something in return—I wanted a baby. I wanted someone to love and love me back. This is never a good reason for bringing a child into a troubled marriage—in fact it's selfish. But I was broken and this is how we think when we're hurting. I thought a baby would ease my pain. In your brokenness you think about what's best for you. You don't consider how it may affect someone else. I never even considered how he would treat a baby.

I started acting like I wanted to have sex with Stanley. He figured out I wanted a baby, so he refused. When he realized he was just denying himself, he stopped resisting and I became pregnant. I thought my pregnancy would make him happy, but I was wrong—he was furious. Later at a religious conference he pushed me and I fell. A few days later I had a miscarriage. After that he refused to be intimate during the rest of our marriage. It was all right because it was torture for me anyway.

Later, I wanted some kind of companionship. So I got a cat and that upset him. One day when I came home the cat began trembling and ran under the bed when she heard his voice. I asked what he had done to her, but he just laughed. Then he picked her up and slammed her against the dresser as hard as he could. My heart ached; she was being abused because I loved her. I couldn't believe this was my life.

The cat limped and ran under the bed. When she finally came out, he was waiting for her. He said I couldn't have her. I cried and cried but he wouldn't let me keep her. I stopped crying when I realized he would only continue to harm her; so I let her go. He took her outside and set her in the driveway. She hung around for a few days, but then I didn't see her again. I could only hope that she found her way into a safe, loving home.

I felt like I had lost another child, and I wanted to die. I couldn't believe a man of God would treat me this cruelly. I've never talked about the cat until now, but it was one more thing I tucked away in my heart of letdowns from God. Sharing my journey with you gives you an opportunity to let God reveal all the hurts you have buried. The key to being free is unlocking the hidden hurts that have held your heart captive.

I don't want to spend any more time on this than I have to, but those women wanted me to understand who they were. If they knew I understood their trials, anger, and fear, they wouldn't have to convince me how hard it is to forgive. But now they could relate to me. I had to learn that trust has to come first in the wilderness of battered hearts before they would listen and follow me. My reason for sharing my shoes with you is so that later, when we get to talking about forgiveness, you'll be ready to hear.

As you begin to start your journey of truth, you will discover what choices you have made that keep bringing you back into your wilderness. I discovered I stopped looking for God to satisfy me before He disappointed me again and so I had begun to put my hope in religion and in relationships. I thought if I got married, I would be complete. This thinking is a trap to set you up in believing marriage quenches your thirsty soul. It can become a god in your life. There is such a high divorce rate because we look at the external and not deal with what's on the inside. Looking back on this journey helped me to see why I had allowed Stanley into my life. The past, where I had been wounded and shaped as a child, was never resolved. My past was always with me; I just didn't realize it. It was in my heart and my thinking.

The elders granted us a separation. I moved out because it

wasn't safe. I was willing to work on the marriage, but I wasn't going to allow him to pounce on me while he figured out his problems. However, I was afraid to divorce him because I thought I would lose my salvation.

The funny thing is, our religion never taught about salvation. There was never any assurance in our relationship with God and where we would spend eternity. It's funny how I could be taught that I am supposed to stay in a relationship no matter what—for good or bad—and that's love. However, they also taught God's love is conditional. They taught only a few chosen were going to heaven, and even they could lose their place. The rest of us hoped to live on paradise. We had to perform works to try to please God. They never showed us God's love—only His laws. On the Day of Judgment we would find out where we would spend eternity. Imagine being taught that you can never feel secure in God's love! So I hadn't wanted a divorce right away because of my religious training. I was in bondage in my thinking and religious beliefs—not so today!

If I divorced Stanley, I would have been shunned, been forced to sit in the back pew, and no one could talk to me. I would not be permitted to remarry, at least not another member. I would be all but cut off from others. This organization had become more than a religion to me; they were my family. So I stayed separated and continued to attend the meetings.

After a few years of living single (as a married person) but without the hope of reconciliation in my marriage, I became discouraged. I wanted to be loved and have children. I had not heard from my estranged husband for over two years—no calls, mail, or financial assistance. The elders never asked me how I was doing. I began to want a divorce but still feared that God would reject me.

I didn't want to believe in the message of this organization anymore. I couldn't accept that the only way I could be loved by God was to stay married to an abusive man. I didn't want to keep living without the possibility of finding love. But then something out of my control happened, which set me free from my religious bondage.

~ 3 ~
God Was Working It Out

I couldn't imagine living like this any longer. At first, I thought keeping busy with the ministry, going from door-to-door, getting up early before I went to work to give out tracts, and having lots of Bible studies, would keep me occupied and feed my soul. Like an alcoholic uses alcohol, I used religion as my fix. Night and day I was consumed with it, so I thought I'd be okay. The problem was that at no time did I call on the name of Jesus. That religion had slipped into His place. I was becoming spiritually dehydrated.

What once filled me with joy and hope no longer satisfied me. I was losing hope in the God who didn't protect me in my childhood and now had me in a holding pattern, living as a married woman without the benefits. I didn't believe in the messages on those tracts anymore. Did God really love me? I was starting to doubt God more and more—not His existence but His goodness, which was much worse.

I didn't know it but God was working things out for me. The problem was, at the time I thought it was one of the most devastating things to happen in my life. I thought it was another sign that He was against me. However, because of my limited ability looking at things in the natural, I couldn't understand how God was working things out on my behalf in the spiritual behind the scenes. This part of writing about the journey was important because it helped me to see how God uses pain to help us. Every painful event I experienced led me to question God's sovereignty in a way that pushed me further away from Him. However, looking back I can truly see the faithfulness of God's promise that He will use the bad things in our lives to work it out for our good. If I had avoided looking at my past, I would have only carried my pain and it would have continued to torment me; I never would have found truth and God again.

One reason why hurting people do not forgive is because their pain deceives them into thinking they shouldn't obey God. This is nothing new. The Bible says the Israelites rebelled against God because they felt like He brought them out into the wilderness to kill them even though He was taking them through the wilderness to get to the Promised Land. The obstacles they were facing made them think God hated them (Deut. 1:26-28 NLT) so their hearts became obstinate toward God and they disobeyed Him. You can't obey or trust someone when you feel they abandoned you in your troubles, including God. Few are just not this honest to confess these feelings toward God, but this is how you get free. Before you can walk in forgiveness, your heart has to be right with God.

I wished He had told me, "Baby girl, I know you think I have left you. I hear you doubting Me and questioning things you can't understand because what I'm doing is so much bigger than you. But trust Me. I'm here; I'm the same God that came to you when you were nine, and I haven't changed. I know you think you have been through so much and you can't take it anymore, but I am God. I created you. I really know how much you can handle. And when you feel like you can't take any more, call on Me and I'll be there. So far, you have just gotten angry or pretended like everything was okay. But know this, baby girl, I see you."

Oh, I wish He had said this to me; but now as I write this He is revealing those moments to let me know He was there. Something was getting ready to unfold that was so painful I almost took my life. I never would have thought He was the one who was behind my escape, but the way it played out, only God could have brought it all together for my good and for His glory.

Purpose in Pain

A friend of mine became angry with me, for what I'll never know. I won't reveal her identity in order to protect her because I love her, and my purpose for sharing this isn't to hurt her. I'll call her Shirley. Someone told her something I supposedly said that made her mad. A close family member told her these things so she was sure it was true. As a result, she wanted me to hurt as much as she had thought I had hurt her.

Shirley and I were very close—like sisters. I never had a conversation with anyone else to hurt her, especially for her to want to destroy my reputation and marriage. This girl was the only person other than God and my mother whom I trusted with my heart. Not even my husband ever had that place.

In my religion if a person wasn't at least trying to become a member, I couldn't really associate with them. Shirley and I were close before I was in this religion or married, and I used to study with her at one time. After I married and relocated, she studied with another Bible teacher in the same religion. Since she continued to study, my husband allowed our friendship before he and I separated. She was the only person he let into my world that I could love. I couldn't use the phone or have family over to my house because they were not a part of the religion. He would take my keys so that I couldn't drive when he wasn't home. He tried to completely control me.

Shirley was my rock, my best friend. When I cried to her, like a baby sister because of the pain I was suffering in my marriage, she would comfort me. When Stanley would beat me, I would call her. She came to me in the night on the streets to find me and get me help. She called my mother for help because I was too ashamed to let anyone know what was happening in my supposedly Christian home. She knew the harm that Stanley could bring to me. What could I have said against her that was worth destroying our friendship, my marriage, safety, and fellowship with God?

She was the only connection I had to the outside world other than Stanley and my religion. Because of the bond we shared, I would have never betrayed her. Shirley and I were kindred spirits. I never laughed as hard or shared my heart with anyone like I did with her. This wasn't a one-sided relationship. She shared her heart and pain with me too. Nevertheless, when she thought I had betrayed her, she wanted to make me pay. Because she was so close to me, she knew exactly what to do—attack me in my religion because at the time that was the key to my faith. She did the unthinkable. She went to her Bible teacher and told her I was having an inappropriate relationship with one of the elders. She says she never said I was having an affair, but what else could they think? In her anger, she wanted to hurt me. It didn't matter if she were wrong.

Not only did I pay for it, an innocent man, one of the elders, was also falsely accused. The man, whom I will call

Luke, was the nicest, godliest, upright man I had met in that whole religious organization. Not once did he ever touch or say anything inappropriately to me. On various occasions I would call Luke, in tears, after one of my husband's explosive temper tantrums. I told him about some of Stanley's harassment: his screaming, breaking up furniture, sitting on me, and not allowing me to go to the bathroom.

See why I didn't want to share my journey? Who wants to share this kind of weakness, pain, brokenness, and foolishness? But I'm doing this for you. It's time to stop hiding behind our pain and being victims to our past. Our past has shaped some of our thinking, but it doesn't have to continue to have power over our identity. God will not let me hold back. Too many people are suffering in silence because they are ashamed to share their pain. You will never get free if you continue to keep inside the afflictions of your soul. This is why you stay tormented and broken and live as victims. It's time to learn how to stand up for yourself and stop allowing your past to shame you. If you shed the light on your darkness, you will take back your power.

My only involvement with Luke was when I called him for counsel and encouragement because no one else would listen. "Keep it hidden, and act like everything is okay" is what people want us to do. People say, "I'm here for you if you need me." But you are judged when you cry out loud. Why can't people be strong and still cry and ask for help? I want you to know you can. God doesn't want you to suffer silently anymore. I really appreciated Luke's caring patience toward me. He never tried to blame me for Stanley's behaviors. He would pray for me, and he would listen.

I wanted to show how thankful I was so I asked Shirley

to help me cook a meal to bless Luke's family. I went to her house to prepare the meal and called Elder Luke to pick it up. Elder Luke and I never went out with each other, nor did I ever make another meal for him. Our only contact was through the organization.

Shirley knew this, but pain and anger were controlling her. She didn't have anyone to show her how to stop. Understanding this journey is important because she didn't know that the anger she was really hurling at me came from something deeper than her thinking I had talked about her. As long as we keep our hurts inside, we stay victims and potential threats to harm others because hurting people hurt other people.

She wasn't trying to destroy my marriage and another person's reputation. She thought she was defending herself, not hurting me. The problem is unresolved pain and anger lead you into a place of darkness, where there isn't light to guide you. If someone had helped her with her pain instead of fueling it, she could have given it to God and we wouldn't have had to go through this mess. However, there was purpose in my pain…

A meeting was called for me to prove that I wasn't having an affair with Elder Luke. My husband was there although we were separated by this time. My husband was my enemy and now my best friend had become my "frien-nemy" even though she knew my life at any time could be in danger or at risk with him.

Back to the Elders

We had the meeting with the elders and I was found innocent of infidelity. After the meeting, the elders wanted to give Stanley and me marriage counseling. But how could they counsel me when they wouldn't listen to where I had been and where I was now—in pain from the abuse? Even if they did know how to make my marriage work, I wasn't going to listen to them because they weren't listening to me. I was tired of Stanley and this organization!

I'm not being rebellious, nor am I suggesting you not allow someone to speak God's counsel into your life. I'm just admitting where I was, and where those classroom women were. I went in trying to teach them before I had taken the time to see where they had been. Then God reminded me how I felt when those religious leaders thought they had the answers for me. They wouldn't talk to me, address my pain, or see me as a person—just give advice. I needed more. I'd been abused, beaten, raped, and slandered, but no one had heard my cry.

On the journey I discovered that a little forgiveness, mercy, and grace is what we all are looking for before we can move on. The ladies in the classes needed a moment to express their pain and be given permission to be angry and help them not sin for the wrong done against them. They needed someone to counsel them who wouldn't become offended or judgmental at their anger but see what caused the pain. Anger is a symptom of the poison inside of you, and they needed to purge it out of their heart.

I couldn't continue going to the place where Stanley and I had attended worship. I didn't want to deal with the rumors or have to face Luke's wife. I put this all behind me and moved on. I never talked about the pain of this experience because Shirley would have been the only one I would have shared it with. I just went to another location and thought all of this was over, but it wasn't. Shirley's thirst for revenge wasn't satisfied so she raised another allegation to her Bible teacher who went to the elders again at my new location, and another meeting was called.

I was devastated to think my friend had done this to me again, but there was nothing I could do. I wished I knew what was said that I had done or what it would take to satisfy her. The elders had to investigate the accusation so I went before a committee and had to prove my innocence again. During our entire separation I believed I was still married in God's sight, so I remained celibate. I did not even date or entertain another man.

I was so hurt to think it was so easy for Shirley to believe a lie against me. I finally realized when you are wounded; it's easier to believe a lie. Then the Holy Spirit whispered in my spirit, "Yes, it is so amazing isn't it, to believe a lie against someone you love and yet this is what my children do to Me all the time." I have to stop and cry for a moment and say, "I'm sorry God for believing a lie and being angry at You after all we've shared."

I'm not carrying my past anymore. Nevertheless, after seeing what Shirley did to me and how I felt, I understand that our pain goes beyond this earth. When the Holy Spirit whispered those words to me, I had only thought about how our pain causes a wedge that separates us from His trust and love. I never thought about the pain we were causing God. Hopefully, after this journey, there will be fewer casualties in your pathway.

In taking this journey, I've been able to remember the pain and anger in my life and see just how deceptive it was. I've been able to see the things I did, the choices I made, and the harm that was done to me because of other's anger. Anger is like a drug—it controls and distorts our perception of ourselves, others, and ultimately God.

In the beginning I really resisted taking this journey. I only wanted to teach from the scriptures and not out of my shoes; I didn't see the reason for it. I thought the past was the problem. As I started the final leg of this journey and talked to more and more people, I see they are thirsty for this journey too. I'm excited for what God is going to do in each and every one of your lives.

Returning to the Journey

Returning to the journey, Shirley thought I had hurt her so she wanted to break me—and it almost worked. A perceived offense became an excuse, which allowed her to behave badly today because of something that hurt her yesterday—and I was caught in the middle. Pain can be fierce, that's why it has to be uncovered, reconciled, and cut down at the root.

The Bible teacher who was studying with Shirley let her know I wasn't punished; the elders didn't believe her story. She wasn't going to stop until she made me hurt as much as she thought I had hurt her. From her standpoint, I didn't suffer any consequences. The funny thing is, how would she know? How can you measure or weigh whose pain is greater? Pain is pain.

What had she lost? I hadn't taken anything from her. She was battling something in her own mind combined with thoughts that were already tormenting her. She couldn't imagine how much I was hurting. I wish she had asked me if I were hurting enough. I wish I knew what it would have taken for her pain to be satisfied. I wish I could have shared the pain in my heart; then she would have known I was bleeding on the inside.

Although Shirley raised these allegations about me to her Bible teacher, Lucy, she was first supposed to come to me. Lucy was my Christian sister, and I knew her. We shared the gospel together, and she didn't even allow me to defend myself. This organization calls themselves the "truth." They even have their own Bible, saying everyone else's translation is wrong. In the Bible it says if a believer sins against you, go privately to him and point out the fault. If they listen and confess it, you have won the person back. If they don't listen, go back and take two or three more people as witnesses. If that doesn't work, then take it to the church before the elders (Matthew 18:16-17). This teacher never came to me. She just listened to Shirley, who wasn't even a member or had any witnesses, and took it to the church.

The day came for me to defend myself again at my new meeting location. I went there with confidence that the elders would see the truth just like before. This time there was only myself and two elders. When they were asking me questions, I could tell they had already made up their minds about me.

At the end of the meeting, the elders wanted to meet again. I didn't know what difference that would make but I agreed. No decision was made that day. When I stood up to leave, I knew I was leaving them forever. Tears began to roll down my face. My heart was so broken I didn't even know if I had enough strength to walk out of there. I didn't know it then, but God used that meeting to set me free from them.

I'd had enough. I didn't care if they were the only way to God. They had let me down. They didn't help me when I was being abused by their minister. As long as I was smiling and handing out their tracts, I was fine to be around, but now I was a problem. They said they were God's faithful and discreet servants. God spoke to their organization personally and yet they couldn't discern the revengeful lies of someone trying to hurt me. They needed to bring Shirley and I together and counsel us to get at the root of her pain and why she was bringing up these accusations.

Up until that point I was afraid to divorce my husband or leave the organization. But now I had had enough. I wasn't afraid. I didn't care what they or God wanted. I was DONE. If God only dwelled within the walls of this organization, they could have Him. He would have to come out and get me if He wanted me back. When I left the meeting, I was desperate, hopeless, and suicidal. God was my everything, but I had to give Him up if the organization was the only way to Him. I didn't have a plan to take my life but I didn't want to live.

I went home and called my aunt and told her I wanted to kill myself. I think I would have, if it hadn't been for her telling my mom what had happened, and she immediately went into prayer for me. I was done with God, but that didn't mean He wasn't God, and He didn't have a plan for my life—I just didn't know it at the time.

I thought God had abandoned me, but now I know He allowed Shirley and her teacher to do this. Otherwise I would have stayed in that organization, under the law of God; never experiencing the love I have with Him now. That was a dark time in my life. I will not deny it. God used it for my good, but it was the most painful time ever in my life.

Returning back to the journey revealed where I lost my

faith. At that point, something just died inside of me, and at that moment I gave up hope. I was tired of defending myself and didn't care anymore. I'm being this transparent about my brokenness because unforgiveness is a powerful stronghold that destroys people. I don't want you to hurt over your past and allow anger to sabotage your blessings. I want you to learn what the enemy really tries to do and how to recover back what was stolen in your past. But you have to stop being emotional and begin to get empowered.

As I look back over these events, I saw God was with me. It's important to see God with you in the wilderness because that's how you begin to start trusting Him again. By their standards the organization never would have believed Shirley over me. Something so impossible could have only been God orchestrating those events. He just wanted me to trust Him, but at the first feeling of pain, I doubted Him instead.

I thought my life was over. Shirley thought she had taken my religion, but she took my God. What was I to do without Him in my life? I couldn't stay in this religion any longer. *Why God? Where are You?* This was how I felt back then. So I understand those of you who question where God is during your trials. But I want you to see He is there—just trust Him. You don't know the whole story yet. God is working it all out for you. I am a living testimony, see my shoes…

Shirley's Story

Before I close this story out I want to share a little more of Shirley's story. Today she and I have reconciled, and I love her and she is my friend. You might be thinking, *How is that possible after all she did to you?* I'm glad you asked.

I've been freed, but she's been carrying guilt. She's been

worrying that I'll stop loving her or being her friend. It's hard for her to trust in forgiveness because it's hard for her to forgive herself or believe I can really forgive her. She's feeling a lot of pain because she believes family members still ostracize her because of what she did to me. Even though I have moved on, she can't; and so we take this journey together.

God is so amazing. I was re-editing this book for the hundredth time, feeling a little overwhelmed about hoping my journey is going to reach hearts the way I believed God intended. I was starting to feel like maybe it's too confusing, when suddenly the phone rang. God sent me a sign to validate the importance of this journey and trust it.

It was Shirley. She said for some reason she couldn't get what happened in our past off her mind. She knew I was writing this book. I had really forgiven her, but she couldn't move forward. She was afraid that other people would influence me to stop being in her life. I loved her with God's love. I had made it through the journey, but she needed reassurance. The only way she was going to get free was to be taken back into the past. At first I reasoned it had happened so long ago there wasn't any reason to bring it up, and it might hurt her. God whispered to me, "No that's a lie. Remember confessing your pain in your past is where healing begins. Then you can begin to forgive." She couldn't even receive my forgiveness until I took her back into the journey. So we finally had the conversation we should have had twenty-eight years ago.

The Conversation

She said, "Tammy, people are mad at me, but they don't know that you talked about me and hurt me. I loved you too.

I forgave you too. But everyone is still mad at me and it's not fair." I didn't want to hurt her but I had to tell her the truth.

I told her, "I allowed you to think you needed to forgive me so that you could move on. But the truth is I never did what you thought I had. I never talked about you to my family member or said the things your Bible teacher had made you think. I loved you with all of my heart. I never stopped loving you. I stopped trusting you but never stopped loving you. You were all that I had. You were the only joy I looked forward to having whenever I was allowed to see you. To hurt you was to hurt me. I'm sorry that you thought I hurt you. I'm sorry that people's jealousy of what we had as friends tried to sever our relationship. The truth is, the reason you hurt me was all based on a lie, and you never even asked me if I said it."

Realizing the pain she caused me and that I really didn't betray our friendship devastated Shirley. It was overwhelming for her to bear. I had to console her and encourage her. This is what forgiveness looks like. The Bible says that you help your brother not to be overcome by their guilt. If we do not help comfort them and encourage them, they will not be able to recover (2 Cor. 2:5-8 NLT). I had to encourage her because I didn't want her to stay stuck. I reassured her again that I loved her and that I had forgiven her.

I asked her why she hadn't come to me to clear up the lies she had been told about me twenty-eight years ago. As she thought about how to answer my question, she discovered something about herself that she was unaware of until she went back into her past. She responded to my question:

"I was beaten by my father for speaking out. So I learned it was better to keep my thoughts or questions to myself.

Funny, I did not realize this until just now; this is the reason why I didn't just ask you. This has always been a problem for me, all of my life growing up. I didn't know how to communicate what I felt, so I struggled with my feelings. I just kept them inside. I was upset about what was put in my mind by others and what others thought of me. I was smart but couldn't read, had three children, and no husband. And when I was told the things they said you had said, I felt like you were ashamed of me. I loved you too."

Now I realize her attack on me twenty-eight years ago was the result of things that had been done to her from her past as a child. She believed I thought poorly of her, and she had other thoughts that gave her low self-esteem. As a child she wasn't permitted to ask questions, so she never learned how to communicate. When she was told I was ashamed of her, it made her think about how her father made her feel about herself. She snapped and let me have what she wished she could have given him.

She reacted because of a wound in her childhood. She carried the pain all those years without any help. This is why we can't ignore the pain in our past. If we don't reconcile it when we are wounded, everyone who comes into our path is a potential target. She didn't realize how healing could have occurred if she had just asked me the question.

False humility (thinking you're unworthy of forgiveness) is really pride or unbelief because it puts you in a position to exalt your thinking above God's and keeps us from receiving His love and forgiveness. I get it when you say you've been beaten over and over again until your pain seems greater than God's voice, but in this journey you'll discover how to make God's voice reign again in your heart.

Shirley didn't discover the answer until twenty-eight years later when she looked into the past to see why she hadn't asked me that all-important question. It's never too late to discover what is keeping you stuck in your pain or preventing you from walking in forgiveness. For Shirley it was fear of her past. I see now why the enemy wants to keep us from going into our past—it holds the key to unlocking our future.

~ 4 ~
God, Where Are You?

The day I walked out of that meeting with the elders, I left and never looked back. I divorced my husband and God. At first everything seemed good. I had my freedom back—I could date and go back to school—the possibilities were endless of what I could do. I reconnected with relationships in my family. I felt like I was able to live and think for myself again.

I lost some weight and started working out and feeling good about myself. I began taking some classes at the Community College. At first I was happy but every so often for no reason a sadness would come over me. I couldn't figure it out at first so I didn't give it much thought. I had my life back and it looked promising. I had family and friends, and I was still young. However, an annoying feeling of melancholy, which I now know was "a spirit of darkness," would come and visit me from time to time, and I didn't know why.

Every once in a while I also would have a desire to want to be with God. I was missing Him, but I was waiting for Him to come to me. I needed proof that He loved me. I didn't want to believe in the organization's teachings anymore, but they remained engrained in my mind. I still believed they were the "truth," as much as I wanted to deny it. I didn't believe God was pleased with any other religion but theirs, even though I experienced what I had.

I was afraid to go to any other place of worship or read any spiritual books or any Bible except for theirs. I was hoping maybe God could have a love affair with me secretly without them knowing and come to me again like He did when I was a child. I wanted Him; I needed Him; I just didn't want that organization. I didn't want to have to prove my heart (my repentance) to a man. I just wanted God, who knew my heart, to show me that He understands.

I waited for God to come but He didn't. Days turned into weeks and months into years. Before I knew it, it had been three years since I had any contact with my Father God. I became angry with God all over again. For a while, I thought time had healed me. I didn't think about how I last felt about God and that He had failed me. However, as more time began to pass, the memory of my pain started to softly remind me that I wasn't free. How could He allow all this time to go by and not try to show me any signs that He still loved me? Was He mad at me because I left the organization or divorced my husband? I needed my God and Father, but where was He?

There was no special person who came into my life that I felt I could love during this time because I was guarded. I wasn't going to allow a man to control me ever again. Stanley had hurt me, and I felt that I would never give another man my trust or heart again. The next man who would come into my life had to be strong and really love me because I was broken and he would have to understand why I couldn't submit under his headship or trust his authority if I became his wife. I'm just being honest, that was how I felt. It wasn't right, but if we can just understand why we reason the way we do before we get married maybe that could prevent some divorces or needless hurts.

During marriage, the pain from our past contributes to those high rates of divorce. It's not that we don't value marriage, we just got married broken and didn't find out what needed to be fixed back in the journey. However, if you're married, instead of keeping secrets and trying to suppress your hurts, open up with each other and share the journey together. Then you will discover the one you love today isn't your enemy in the relationship. You're holding one another hostage for the enemies from your past. Finding God's love is the solution; however, you will never understand that kind of love until you surrender your pain to Him.

The past left me twisted in my thinking toward future relationships; it was wrong. Pain doesn't have the right to make someone else pay for the mistakes of another person from our past. On the other hand, to show His love for us, Jesus paid the price with His life and spared our life to bear our sins on the cross. That's the love that God has for us (John 3:16), and the power of love and grace available to heal our brokenness so that no one has to bear others' crosses.

All men are not as bad as Stanley; he was broken. I just didn't want to see it before I married him. The truth is real love will never guide you to a place of darkness where someone abuses, betrays, or misuses you. Today I have taken responsibility not for what he did, but in my choice to allow him to do it. When we are in pain, we have to confess it and get free so that anger doesn't take root in our hearts and we give place to the enemy to separate us from God (Eph. 4:24-26). Anger is what gives the enemy access to us and takes us into a place of darkness and deception because the source of light is gone.

The light had almost flickered out. But thank God I had experienced His touch enough to want it again. The enemy couldn't deceive me anymore to think life was okay without God in my life. There was no pain great enough or excuses good enough to keep me from going to God. I finally couldn't take being away from God any longer—not another day, moment, or second. My insides were going to burst if I didn't cry out to my God. I didn't know if He cared or would listen, but I needed Him. I didn't know what to say. I want you to know there is no right or wrong way to speak to Him other than simply opening your mouth and sharing what is in your heart. No one else can tell your story.

It was time for me to have my Job moment. God wants a broken and contrite heart—one that's ready to listen to Him and not rely on human reasoning to know whether His wisdom is satisfactory. He wants a surrendered heart—one that is ready to hear Him—a heart that will allow Him to be God in your life despite your perception of Him because of your circumstances.

He hadn't come to me sooner because He waited until I was ready to allow Him to be God. Until this point I wanted Him to prove to me He was God based on my definition and expectations. I would have still been trying to make Him subject to me. That's why we can't get free. But now I was ready, and He knew it because He saw into my heart.

I didn't know how to start the conversation. Do I say, "Hi, God; it's me, Tammy; long time no hear"? How do you begin a conversation with the God you turned your back on? I think the best way is in humility. Just be you. So I just cried out, "God!" That's all it took. He had been waiting for me all along.

A Job Moment

What is a Job moment? Remember Job was the man in the Bible whose children were all killed at once; he lost his wealth and health, his wife told him to curse God, his family abandoned him, and his friends judged and blamed him for his circumstances. He was trying to talk it out with them at first. They all knew what he had experienced—they knew the events since that was probably the biggest news of the time back then.

They may have said something to others like, "Hey, did you hear about Job? He's supposed to be so blameless and up-right. He thought his kids were all of that, even making sac-rifices for them to God while they were adults. He and his family were supposed to be the pillars of the religious com-munity. Look at them now. I guess the truth will eventually come out and show what is really going on behind closed doors. All the sermons he preached and his giving to the poor made him look like he was so righteous. I guess God showed that he really was a hypocrite—no better than anyone else. He was always preaching for us to live holy. Now look at him—no one is going to listen to him."

They judged him because of his circumstances so they couldn't have had a heart of compassion during his troubles. They had never experienced what he just went through so they couldn't be empathetic. And the others were jealous so they hid their joy at his misfortune and gave him heartless counsel.

But Job was desperate. He needed help. He didn't know

who to turn to at first. He thought he could cry out to his godly friends. However, because of how they were responding to his pain, he saw that they were the wrong people to listen to (Job 6:26 NLT). So he kept crying until his cries reached heaven. He was now in the presence of God.

What did he do? This is so important. I used to hate reading the book of Job—thirty-eight chapters of reading about a man's suffering and complaining was hard to relate to. Every year when I would read the Bible, I would skim over or entirely skip the book of Job. Finally one year when I began seriously finishing this book, God showed me why I didn't want to read Job. The enemy was keeping me from the treasure in it that had the answer for why we need to cry and take our pain to God.

I finally looked at what Job was saying to God and ignored his friends, the debaters. (I won't share too much. You can read the book for yourself. I recommend that you read it with fresh eyes and allow it to be another part of showing you how to bare your soul before God and get free. I will just share a few things that Job said to God that reveal the darkness that was in his heart and how pain had twisted a blameless righteous man's perception of a God who had once held a special place in his life.)

Job asked God why He didn't just come down and kill him. He said that he wished he would have been a stillborn, that no light should shine on his birthday, and his birth date should be removed off the calendar and cursed. He said that his mother's womb should have been cursed for having him. (I'm adding this because I want you to know what pain does to us, even to those who love God. Stop holding it in and don't allow anyone to stop you [Job 3:1-11, 6:1-8 NLT]).

Imagine if he had kept those feelings inside—they were poison for his soul, eating him alive. He had to get that junk out of him. You cannot bear anything good in your life with those kinds of feelings. They will separate you from God. Oh the enemy tries to distract us for a while with glamour, status, sex, drugs, alcohol, relationships, and anger, but eventually when you are alone with your thoughts, the Holy Spirit will whisper to you and remind you of Himself. He exists no matter how we try to ignore Him. The glory of God is all around us. Despite the rainbows, sunrises, changing of the seasons, birth of babies, or small miracles we encounter, we try at times to discredit Him.

Something else I want to remind you is that the enemy was there all along during Job's circumstances. Some of you may not like to know this, but God allowed Satan to test Job. He had to be given permission. God in His wisdom knew why He allowed it, and at the end Job was blessed and had restored all that was lost. (I can't go deeper into why God allowed this because I'd start writing another book within this one.) However, the reason I bring Satan up is because I want you to understand what you have had to endure really is a spiritual battle. Many times we get mad at God and people, but we leave the enemy out.

The enemy was there and never left, influencing Job's friends to say some of the things they said to accuse Job. The enemy accuses us day and night. He wants us to distrust God's love and word, and accuse each other. But the biggest evidence that the enemy was there was the darkness, suicidal thoughts, and even a desire to have God kill you. When you have these kinds of thoughts, beware that these thoughts are not yours—they are the enemy's. He tries to use your circumstances to get you to think like him, exalt your thinking above God's, and believe the lies of deception (2 Cor. 10:3-5).

It's important to know the enemy is present in your pain because that's who's feeding your heart to stay angry. As long as you stay angry, he will stay nearby. Anger is the gate to your heart. The way to get rid of the anger starts in reconciling and confessing the pain. Confess it and tell God what is hurting you. You can't be angry about something that you no longer are hurting over. You confess the pain because anger lingers where there is unresolved pain. All the hurt will not dissolve immediately, but you will have begun the healing process.

Job was relentless. He didn't let his family, friends, church leaders, anger, or the enemy stop him from getting his pain out. He showed us why we need to confess our pain before God and why sometimes people can't help us. Going to God allowed him to be in a position to see truth despite being controlled by his emotions. So I followed Job and had my moment. I allowed all that stuff that I had been carrying for those three years to come out. I asked some questions and accused Him of some things. He allowed me to go on until I was finished.

When I cried out to God at this point, I felt His presence, His peace, and that familiar comfort I had longed for and hadn't felt in years. I felt His warmth. I didn't feel guilt or condemnation. I felt an indescribable sense of love. I began to ask God questions that had been on my heart, things I had been carrying, which is how you begin to let go of the past. For instance, I asked, "My mother said you were my Father, what kind of Father are you, God? You could have stopped some of my pain…. Why did you stop loving me, God?"

That was how I was feeling and I needed to get it all out, no holding back. You have to be completely willing to be honest before God if He's going to help you. Otherwise, the enemy will later torment you with what you try and keep hidden.

I'm not saying everything that happens to you will cause you to be angry with God or question His sovereignty and love. But if something does, you'll not be free from that situation until you confess it. Don't be afraid to admit that you're angry with God. Jesus even had to send a message back to John the Baptist when he was in prison, saying, "Blessed is the man who is not offended by the Son of Man." Even John had become upset with Jesus because when John was in prison, facing death, Jesus didn't come and change his circumstances. We get stuck when we judge God's sovereignty by how we feel He should work out our situation. He wants us to trust Him to work it out.

I know this is hard. I'm not trying to be entertaining. This was my life. I forgot that I had been there in that dreadful, dark, lonely place. I can't believe I ever allowed pain and my lack of wisdom to take me out of a place of light, truth, and love, but I did. I said to God, "You have not been a God, Father, or Protector to me." Can you imagine thinking that way about God? I think a lot of you have felt this way a time or two. In fact until you are honest about your anger toward God, it will continue to remain a stumbling block and hinder you from moving forward. You can't follow Him if you're mad at Him.

During most of my childhood, I felt alone. Although I had siblings, we weren't close. I was molested. My best friend betrayed me, and my father rejected me. All of my life I wanted to feel loved. More than anything in life, I just wanted a family. I asked God why He didn't stop me from marrying Stanley. I really cried my heart out to God so that He could see inside of me. I felt betrayed by God because no one, not even Him (I thought), had loved enough or protected me. When you go to God, He hears, and He will respond, although you may not always like the answer. After I had my fit, He was ready to answer me.

Suddenly God whispered, "You had free will to marry, but you never asked Me." I couldn't get mad; He was right. I didn't ask anyone for advice. I probably wouldn't have listened. I wouldn't have believed I was getting ready to make such a huge mistake. I was all of 19 and I thought I knew everything. He also said If I had been in His love the way I professed, I would've known that what I was getting into wasn't love. Ouch!

Why Confess the Pain

God will answer some of your questions, especially those that will get you to open your mind to truth. He will respond to those questions that will allow you to know that He is God and you can't deny it despite your pain. He will answer those questions that will allow you to see yourself against Him and realize you can't question His wisdom. Finally, He will answers those questions you need to have answered to move on, humble yourself, and get back into a place of worship with Him again.

God took Job through a series of questions asking where Job was when He laid the foundations of the earth, who set the boundaries of the seas and did he know their depth, and where does light come from. He asked Job how snow and hail is made, who created the channel for torrents of rain, and can he hold back the movement of the stars (Job 38). God made Job take his focus off of his pain once he had gotten it out. You don't confess it to stay stuck in it—you confess it to get your eyes and heart off your circumstances and back on God. Our perception can be altered because of the pain, so we need to get it out. God doesn't want us to stay connected to it. Once we confess our pain, we can lay it down. Then God brings our eyes back on to Him so we can see the truth and light about Him again.

When God asked Job all of those questions that only God could answer, Job was able to see the sovereignty and majesty of God again. His pain was confessed, and it no longer was consuming him. His heart was lighter, so he was able to get his eyes off himself and put them back on God above. His anger was no longer able to deny the power of God. Therefore he couldn't deny the love of God either since he was in His presence. Without anger feeding his soul, he no longer was in darkness. God is love, so no longer could he possibly think God took pleasure in his suffering or wanted to kill him.

Anger is broken when you really get in the presence of God. At that point the enemy's hold on us is broken. Where there is a heart of reverence, worship, and repentance, the enemy has to flee from us (James 4:7). Pain separates us from God and makes us think God left us. Job had humbled himself by admitting that he tried to questioned things about God he did not know or understand.

He said he had heard about God before, but now he'd seen Him with his own eyes (Job 42:5 NLT). All the riches, prestige, position, and family that he had previously enjoyed never allowed him to see God before the way that only his experience of pain now allowed. Some things and places we will never experience except we go through suffering, and God knows what pain will get us to our destiny. We have to trust Him.

Job saw how awesome the Creator is. God's presence humbled him and made him realize his pain could no longer dethrone God. He lifted his eyes to the heavens and placed God back on the throne. My eyes are filled with tears because I didn't learn this until I saw it through healed eyes and not a broken heart.

Job had his own questions he had to ask before he saw God as greater than his pain. What questions do you have? So what worked for me? I needed to know God loved me and He addressed it. He said, "I do love you. I never stopped loving you, and I never will stop loving you. It would be impossible for Me not to love you because I AM LOVE."

Up until that point I was never sure of His love. Read the following scripture like a love letter from Jesus, Father God, and the Holy Spirit:

Can anything ever separate us from Christ's love? Does it mean he no longer loves us if we have trouble or calamity or are persecuted or are hungry or cold or in danger or threatened with death?(Even the scriptures say, "For your sake we are killed every day; we are being slaughtered like sheep"). No despite all of these things overwhelming victory is ours through Christ who loves us. And I am convinced that nothing can separate us from his love. Death can't and life can't. The angels can't and the demons can't. Our fears for today and our worries about tomorrow, and even the powers of hell can't keep God's love away from us. Whether we are high above the sky or in the deepest ocean, nothing in all creation will ever be able to separate us from the love of God that is revealed in Christ Jesus our Lord (Rom. 8:35-39).

This was the assurance I needed (and probably many of you do too) when I questioned how can a loving God allow bad things to happen. I just had to accept that despite whatever happens to us, nothing but our hearts can separate us from God. He never left us. I know it's hard to understand why He allows things to happen as He does. However, this walk is a love walk; He doesn't ask us to understand, just to trust and obey Him, and believe that He will use it for our good (Rom. 8:28). Love will motivate you to obey His word and forgive. After you've addressed your pain and had your throw down with God, you no longer need to be preoccupied with it. Pain doesn't have to dominate you. You're ready to move to the next phase.

I wanted to finish this journey. I thought I had shared enough. I was ready to start teaching on forgiveness, but God kept whispering to me to share the whole story. "You have made it through the journey. Help my people understand how they got stuck in the beginning. What's weighing them down? The pain that they're carrying isn't just from today. Show them what has shaped them. Where did it all start? Then they can really learn from their past and not bring their past into today. Then they will know how to 'let go and let Me.' Give them the rest of your story."

~ 5 ~

What Has Your Heart Bound?

God still had some stuff He wanted to reveal to me about what was hurting me. Although I had confessed a lot to Him already, He let me know there was more unfinished work to be done. In this next phase I was going to get my breakthrough, get healed, and be able to show others how to get delivered. I had to be able to show the women that the journey really started before I had married Stanley or became tangled up with a controlling religion that I made my God.

God was leading me to share a little more with the women, but I was resistant. I had already shared more things than some of them cared to know or have ever heard from their spiritual leader. God whispered to me, "This isn't just about you, My child; it is for My other family (sons and daughters) who are still crying and looking for Me. You have to show them how you really got lost and how you found Me again. Then they will know too."

I wondered what else in my past I would have to share. At this point I was exhausted so I had to get some rest and go to sleep. As I was trying to sleep, God was constantly bringing up visions and memories of when I was a little girl.

"Daddy, Daddy!" I was calling out in a dream, tossing and turning. In the dream I was a little girl who was scared and crying out for a daddy, but then I remembered I didn't have one. A sadness and darkness came over me in my dream, and that memory caused me to cry. When I awoke I had real tears streaming down my face. As a child I knew my father never accepted me, but I was a grown woman so I wondered what that had to do with anything.

I always wanted a dad, someone to run to for safety. I wanted to jump into his arms and feel secure, beautiful, and see the light in his eyes because he was captivated by his little girl. I wanted to make him feel ten feet tall because his little girl thought he was the most important person on the earth, and I wanted him to captivate my heart too.

When I was a child, I wished I had a father like other kids, so I would dream that I had a dad, but when I would awake and remember it was a dream, I would carry a little sadness in my heart. I acted like it didn't matter not having a dad, and I never shared this with anyone. I knew my dad, but I never knew why he seldom had anything to do with me. Why didn't he love me or my mother? I wrestled with those questions in my mind often until I went to sleep. I had forgotten about that hurt. It's amazing how I thought this was all about a class teaching others, but God was using it to reveal truth to me. Not that I was walking in unforgiveness, but to be honest I didn't know how I had arrived at some of those dark places in my heart or mind back then until I started the journey. I just knew I had landed there. What I thought I was doing to help others shed some light on my own story.

As a child I loved watching Shirley Temple movies. She often played an orphan or someone separated from her father, and I would be glued to the television, filled with anticipation as she tried to be reunited with her father. I would be crying more than she would. I always rejoiced over her finding her father because I had hoped one day my father would come and find me.

I never had the pleasure of ever calling a man daddy except my maternal grandfather. I didn't really have a close relationship with my father so when he did come by for a visit, I could only call him by his name. I wasn't trying to be disrespectful, but my heart couldn't call him Daddy. I didn't experience that privilege until my early thirties when we finally connected, and I will forever be grateful. It took a long time in coming, but it was still worth it.

My biological father and mother didn't marry so I never really knew him as a child. I saw him a few times here and there in crisis moments. But my mother, discerning how much a father meant to me, told me that God was my Father, and I took it seriously. I wanted to know my Father (God), and so I talked with Him. I would say, "If You are my Father, God show me." And then one day I felt an overwhelming presence of God. It was Him and He came to visit. I was too young to discern how to communicate with the Spirit, but He loved me enough to let me know He was there. From that moment on, I stopped having nightmares about not having a daddy because I had the best daddy of all—God Almighty. At the time, I thought He was all mine so it was really special. I thought the God of the heavens loved me so much that He came to only me to replace my father in my life.

A few years later my heavenly Father answered my prayer and gave my mother a husband. I can't remember now if I ever called him dad, but I know in my heart I thought of him as dad. I was so excited to have a dad. In the beginning my stepfather was very loving toward my mother and her five children. Having him in my life was the closest resemblance to a father and a complete family we had ever had. He worked hard and was a good provider. He and my mother had one child together, but he treated all of us the same. He acted like he loved us, and I loved him.

Some of my happiest holidays were because of him. I don't know when my mother fell in love with him, but I knew when I did—when he brought all of us beautiful Easter outfits. That was the first time I felt like a princess from my head to my feet. I had never been so dressed up as a child. I had a new hat, dress, gloves, purse, and shoes. I never felt as pretty as I did that day. I twirled around like Shirley Temple in my pretty dress and saw the sparkle in his eyes as his little girl captivated him. Seeing him look at me with such a big warm smile touched my heart, and I let him completely inside my heart. He was my dad whether or not I uttered the words or not.

For Christmas my stepfather Terry brought all of us bikes. He had a smile as big as the word Christmas and a heart to match it. He was so good to my mother and us in the beginning. Home felt like home because of him. I hadn't seen my mother as happy as she was with him. We always had family gatherings over at our house, and my mom didn't have to work. In the beginning, he loved my mom and my brother and sisters like we were his own, but then it all changed when he began to use drugs.

God had been bringing up specific memories, and so far, the past seemed all right, but the sweet memories began to fade and I saw why He brought me back into this place. This is truly the place where it all started—where I lost my trust and belief in God's love for me. This is where my heart was broken, and my understanding of what love means became distorted. I was never the same again. My innocence was taken and the enemy tried to rob me of my identity.

Terry began molesting me when I was about eleven or twelve. At first, it was very subtle. He would make little sarcastic remarks about my body as he teased me because I was starting puberty. Then he began touching my breast, but he did it in front of everyone, saying, "Look at the bumble-bee pimples on your chest," and joking around. I didn't think anything of it at first, other than he was annoying me, and everyone would laugh and say, "Stop poking fun of her."

However, things began to progress. I would find him looking at me in a way that made me feel uncomfortable. He started caring too much about what I wore. Once he didn't like a shirt I was wearing. It was an African Dashiki shirt, nothing revealing. He wanted to control what I wore. It had a little slit at the breast, but I didn't really have breast, so what difference did it make? He slapped me and made me change.

Then he repeatedly came into my room to fondle my body, kiss me, and pull my underwear off or put my hands on his genital area. Thankfully I was able to fight and prevent him from having sex. I shared a room with my other sisters, and he knew I wasn't afraid to scream, but it was a daily battle. As soon as everybody went to bed, he would come up into my room and attempt to get in bed with me, trying to tear my panties off. I would scream and he would run out of my bedroom. I don't know if my sisters heard or were too scared to say anything or really were asleep because we never talked about it.

For months I wore extra clothing to bed and wrapped extra blankets around me so that when he entered my room, I would feel him pulling at the covers and I would awake. No one found it strange that I had lots of covers on my bed even though it was warm weather. In addition to trying to sleep with me almost every night, he became abusive toward my mother. It was so embarrassing leaving the house for school because I knew the neighbors had heard all the screaming and fighting and saw the police cars come and go. I hated him for what he was doing to my family: hurting my mother, trying to have sex with me, and all the while trying to act like he was the perfect person.

I was afraid that someday my screams wouldn't stop him. My screams were turning into violent threats. I was going to have to follow through with them to make him know I wasn't scared of him, but what could I do? I was a little skinny girl fighting against a six foot plus man. I thought about sleeping with a knife but was afraid he might use it against me. So I made the decision to confront him in front of my mother. He denied my accusations and she believed him. My mother thought I just didn't want her to be happy. She thought that I was being defiant toward my stepfather's authority because she thought I did not like him. She told me and my stepfather to work out our differences, that we were a family and must learn to live together.

Sometimes when my stepfather was abusive toward my mother, I would jump in the middle of it and defend her. I even threatened him that I would kill him or cut off his body parts. She didn't understand where such anger was coming from. How could I say such disgraceful, nasty words toward him? I looked awful. She didn't understand just because she didn't believe me that it didn't mean it wasn't true. I had pain and darkness in me. What's in the heart comes out of the mouth. He had betrayed my trust. He was killing my spirit. He was stealing my identity. He had stolen a father's love from me, which originally was an answered prayer. He had captivated my heart and now he was perverted. I couldn't be the innocent, loving child that God had created me to be. I had to be prepared to fight.

My mom didn't realize when I stood in the middle of their disputes to defend her that I was defending me too in front of her. I needed to go to a different place to show him that I wasn't afraid of him. I thought with me making those threats toward him in front of my mother, I had help whether she understood I was using her support for my battle or not. I was trying to stand tall in front of my mother so he would know that I wasn't going to let him defeat me when he come after me in my bedroom.

First, I want to say if my mother ever thought this was true, she never would have allowed this or turned a blind eye. My mother is like a lion for her children and always has been. However, she didn't believe me because she saw my anger and it overshadowed my pain. My anger looked like disrespect to her. She saw it and thought I must be trying to find a way to get rid of him because I had told her repeatedly to leave him because of their fights.

I'm not trying to excuse her for not believing me—it crushed me, and it took a long time for me to get over it, but I want you to know there is a reason why we do and think the way we do. My mom thought I was just meddling in her business. Even though my stepfather had changed, and he wasn't the same, loving protecting man toward her or us, she

What's in the ❤ comes out of the mouth

was holding on to hope that he would become that same man again. I get that. As an adult you have the right to decide if you want to make a relationship work. In some regards, a child has no right to stand in the middle and be disrespectful, making derogatory remarks toward their parents.

Nevertheless, for any parent reading this who may have children and you find yourself in a similar situation where your child tells you someone is hurting them and you don't believe them—ask yourself what is causing such fear and anger to rise up in your child. Is it worth it to take the chance that maybe you are sleeping with a molester? How do you know who's telling the truth? I understand that some children do lie, and they want to destroy your home; but even if this is the case, a child who would go to those extremes to break up a loving home is still broken and needs someone to see their "cry," their pain, and not just their behavior through their anger. What is making them lie? Children are suffering, and the pain of what happened to them continues through generations down through the families. Investigate your children's cries. It isn't enough to just ask a question.

Too many children are being molested, raped, sodomized, and beaten. I know some of you mothers didn't know about it, and this is not a guilt trip. Rather this is a journey to get healed for all of us. Now isn't the time for blame. However, I ask you if your child has ever told you they were molested or raped or abused and you didn't believe them, would you just look into your child's eyes and investigate the truth?

Our daughters are not just getting raped. Our sons are getting raped, and they are growing into angry men who don't know how to love women. Some have become abusive because they feel they have to prove their masculinity. Some have become confused in their sexual identity, and it has become a struggle in their life because of a sin done against them in the past. Many keep silent and stay tormented from these desires because they are ashamed, and they condemn themselves for the sins done against them.

Those same little abused children who had no one to protect them are hiding inside the hearts of angry adults today, causing a lot of emotionally underdeveloped adults to bring a lot of hurt into their relationships. It's not too late; I promise. No matter what trauma, pain, or suffering you experienced as a child, if you confess it today, you can get healed. Please, it's time to get free. If you know people who have been abused, stop seeing their anger and help them in their pain. Once they reconcile with their pain, there will be no place for anger or for the enemy to have a mighty place to deceive and use them against themselves. Without anger, light comes in, along with love and forgiveness.

You can get help right here if you confess your pain, confess what it has done to you, and give it to God. Trust Him and let Him in, and stop making Him subject to you. You can get healed right now. Let your family in to help you if you have been carrying this secret that is tormenting you from your past.

By taking this journey and giving your pain and anger to God, you can let it go once and for all, instead of hiding it, ignoring it, or belittling it. You need to shut the door so those same uncles, fathers, and stepfathers, whoever has violated you, can't come into your daughters' and sons' lives.

The reason for my story is to help readers get to a place where they are willing to be honest about what's really hurting them. Pray and ask God to reveal where life changed you so you can begin to come out from underneath the lies about what happened to you, what people think about you and what you think about yourself, God, and others.

Twisted Thinking

I know it was hard for my mother to believe my stepfather was this kind of man, but it was true. She thought I hated him, but I didn't—I loved him. He was the only real father that I had had. She saw the external blessings he was providing for us, but she didn't realize the internal blessings he was robbing from us. She couldn't know the identity he was trying to steal from me: my self-worth, security, confidence, and the joy of a father's love that I had prayed for. I know my mother never would have allowed anyone to hurt her children and yet for some reason she couldn't see that I was telling the truth. How was that possible when he even hurt her? She saw his anger and my anger, and some kind of way when they both were lined up against each other; she believed his story over mine.

My mother thought she could separate how Terry interacted with her and us. She thought if they had their fights or arguments, it didn't affect us. But it did and it caused me to think differently toward him before he even started to act inappropriately toward me. I couldn't separate how he treated her. I couldn't turn my heart on and off. If you hurt my mother, you hurt me.

This is when the pain became lodged in my heart. I was willing to stand up for my mother. I was willing to take a beating for her. It never came down to taking it physically, but I would have. I would have done anything to protect her. I didn't want anyone to hurt her even if she trusted them; my guard was up. But where was her guard for me? From that point on, life didn't matter to me anymore. There was no one to show me that I was worthy of their love. This is what pain was telling me. If I had been able to, I could have opened my heart up and got that lie out. I would not have taken this deceptive thinking into my future where wolves were lurking to mislead me and take advantage of a vulnerable heart. This is where my past had shaped me.

My stepfather's inappropriate attention toward me caused me to have a lot of issues with my body and issues with my beauty. It wasn't something I wanted to embrace. I had problems with intimacy later in life, but sex was easier because I could be in control without getting my heart involved. Although Terry, my stepfather, never had sex with me, it took a while before my opinion of sex changed from feeling it was something dirty to something that could be enjoyed as a marital experience.

A father's love is what helps you to trust, feel secure, and be confident to live outside in society. Apart from knowing who you are in God, I think a father's love is the next most defining. I lost the security in my home so I didn't know how to trust. So when someone says let go and let God, that's like speaking a foreign language without an interpreter. What does all of that spiritual jargon mean? Trust the God who did nothing and watched it happen? This is why I hope this journey walks you through how to let go…

A father has a way of making you feel like the spotlight is on you and you're special no matter what you are doing. When that doesn't happen, you spend your life searching for something to fill you and make you feel loved. Always searching outside of yourself because you lack completeness is a dangerous place in which to be. It's tragic to grow up without a father's real love. I made many poor choices because of that, including marrying someone who abused me. If I had understood this back then and taken this journey into my past, I could have possibly prevented that mistake.

At first my anger was just directed toward my stepfather, but when my mother didn't believe me and even suggested that we try to work out our differences, at that moment I hated her too. But that was a wounded child reacting. So I ran away from home to live with my grandparents. Again my mom just thought my leaving was because I was a rebellious child and that I didn't want to live with her. I hated that she never realized that I was hurting, and I loved her more than anything. I was leaving because I was in danger and needed some place safe where I could feel loved.

I went to live with grandparents. I told them what had been going on and they believed me, but nothing happened. We didn't talk about it further. No one asked if I was all right or how had this affected me. No one checked on my heart. People don't understand that your circumstance and how it affects you are entirely two different things. They told me I had to put it behind me and not talk about it anymore. It's ironic that we are taught that the solution to our pain is to hide it, keep things secret, just ignore what just happened, and magically all the darkness held inside will not affect your inner being.

My grandparents loved me. I'm so thankful for them. I stayed with them for several years. They always welcomed me anytime I needed to come back there; it was always home. They didn't know any better back then they didn't talk about such things. Nevertheless, as well intended as people have been in your life, if you experienced pain and they hugged you but didn't allow you to fully express and identify what happened to you, they have helped you to become stuck in your past. We need hugs and an open safe environment in which to have honest conversations.

When many people think of pain, it has to be tangible in order for them to understand. However, what affects your body affects your mind and soul. My soul was hurting; it's true you will heal because of physical trauma, but the longer you delay confessing and reconciling with the emotional pain from the trauma, you will never be whole. You can't move on this way. You can't run from your own mind because the thoughts of pain continue to follow you.

My mother had told me that God was my heavenly Father. I believed that but what was the point if He stood by and did nothing? That reasoning and thinking began to leave a void in my heart between God and me for many years. I never had anyone to ask about why God allows bad things to happen to the ones He said He came to save. I didn't have anyone to help walk me through my pain, so it followed me into my future. I stopped trusting God as my Father. Those were the feelings I had had as a child. And just because time had passed, those feelings were still there, but I just didn't know it. I had gotten good at hiding my heart and just moving on with a smile. We're deceived in thinking we're fine because we lived through our past, but we fail to realize the past is still inside of us until we confront it.

I lived with my grandparents and they took good care of me. Unforgiveness had begun to lodge in my heart because anger had taken root. No one helped me to unmask my pain. A change of place doesn't take away anger. It may temporarily take away your focus, but it will still be there until you confess it. There is no forgiveness in the midst of anger. You have to make a choice to surrender to one or the other. Where there is unforgiveness, there is no God for He says light and darkness cannot reside together.

I didn't say you can't believe in God where there is unforgiveness. I'm saying God will not be where there is no forgiveness; it doesn't matter who is at fault. He just says fix it, forgive, and make it right, and then there will not be anything preventing you from having access into His presence. I now know that the master plan of the enemy is to keep anger in our hearts because he knows that unforgiveness keeps us away from God, His power, love, and the blessings at His altar (Matt.5:23-25). The reason you feel so hopeless, powerless, and depressed is because without God present, there isn't any power to forgive. The enemy wants to keep you away from God and will try to use any yoke including pain to detain you from returning there.

After about a year, I started to miss living at home with my siblings and my mother. We would still see each other at family dinners, picnics, barbeques, and it looked like everything was okay. None of my other sisters ever said our stepfather had tried anything with them, and they said he wasn't fighting our mother anymore. They looked happy. So I wanted to be back with my family. I was willing to forgive Terry, and I loved my mom.

I returned home. For the first few weeks, my mom slept in my room with me to help me feel comfortable. Everything was going wonderfully. My stepfather was acting nice toward me, not resentful or indecent. We were all happy. So my mother returned back to their bedroom and that same night he returned to mine. It was raining and thundering fiercely that night. It almost was like a sign for the prelude of what was about to happen. I couldn't believe that he would try this again. He came into my room completely naked, which he had never done before. He came over to my bed, and I was so afraid. I wasn't prepared to fight him; my guard was let down. I had trusted him again so it was unexpected. I didn't have the extra clothes or blankets. I thought I had my father again. I had forgiven him, and I thought I would be safe. Isn't that what we are taught? Forgiveness makes everything better. What happened?

Thank God my mother had her guard up. For some reason either she decided to follow behind him this time or she noticed he wasn't in the bed and went to see where he was. Although he was standing over my bed completely naked, soon she would be coming to my rescue. He hadn't ever been this bold before. I guess he figured no one believed me so he didn't have anything to lose. I was so terrified. Just as the lightning was thundering through the sky with all its fierce power, I was desperately trying to hold onto the covers to prevent him from getting in bed with me.

As Terry and I were tussling back and forth with the covers, out of nowhere my mom burst into my room like a powerful human bolt of lightning. She demanded, "Why are you in her room?" I thought, *Oh here we go again. Please don't believe him, Mommy. Put me first. Save me. Heavenly Father are You looking at what's happening this time? Are You going to protect me? Will she believe me?* Then my stepfather answered, "I just wanted to check on the kids since it was a storm." She said, "Not naked!" She jumped on top of him, beat him on the head with the broom, and all of us bit him, kicked him, and pushed him down the stairs. I want to say we threw him out of the house that instant, but I can't remember if she allowed him to get his clothes on or not. I know that was the end of him. He was never ever allowed to come back into our lives.

I was so proud of my mother because she fought for me and had protected me! I thought I could open up my heart again, and things would be different. We were finally going to be a happy family. I thought my mother would hug me, comfort me, and say she was sorry that she hadn't believed me. I thought she would at least ask if I were okay. No, once again I just had to continue to hold back my pain. I had to hold it all in and keep quiet, think about others, and act like what just happened never did. This type of circumstance causes some of you not to want to forgive. You feel like someone let you down or you wonder if anyone thought about you. But keep following me because God's love does work—it never fails.

God Is a Loving God

God is so loving—more than we can ever know. I had no idea when I started teaching that class all those years ago why He had me go back into the past. It was all about love. We have been saying, "God, where are you?" We have felt like He wasn't with us in our pain or somehow didn't see us. Often we felt compelled to tell God our pain because we didn't think He was aware of it. But my God has allowed me to go back so that I could show you that in the midst of our storms, He will provide a way for escape for you. He was there all along.

God allowed me to return back to my past so I could

allow you to see how in the midst of our pain, we think He has abandoned us. He wanted to show you what has shaped your thinking that caused your perception of Him to be distorted. He was there; he didn't allow Terry to rape me. And for you who were raped, I'm sorry but it still doesn't mean He wasn't there; you're going to just have to look in your story and see how He was there with you. He allowed a place for me to go when I needed my grandparents. And when I needed my mother, God put something in her to move her to come into my room.

You have to look for those God moments. He may not have come the way you wanted or when you desired, but keep trusting Him. This is the purpose of the journey. God doesn't want pain and anger following us around all our lives. He wants us to learn some lessons and see Him truly as God. The wilderness of trials was supposed to show us that despite anything we encountered, God was able to provide for and deliver us. The wilderness was designed to strengthen us so that when the enemy tries to tempt us to resist God and doubt His love, we would remain steadfast and not turn away in our hearts (Matt. 4:1-10). The wilderness was supposed to be a passing journey; it was never intended for us to make it our home.

After that night, I had to just move on. I was glad my mother stood up for me, but she didn't check my heart. I don't know why. I couldn't just be happy that she had fought for me. Now I was mad that she didn't say, "I'm sorry, baby, you were telling the truth. Everybody thought you were just a rebellious girl who wanted to have her own way, but what you said was true. Are you all right?" Even if she never said that, if she would have said, "I love you" and just held me, it would have been okay. But no, we went to bed, and I went to school the next day and we never talked about it. I became an angry, bitter teenager. And I didn't understand this was what shaped me. I loved my mother, but after this I became disrespectful. Unfortunately people still just look at your behavior and not your heart.

I was vulnerable now, prey for anyone or anything that would give my heart attention. This was how I became involved with that organization and eventually had a blind spot about love to allow Stanley to come into my life.

On the outside I looked like I had adjusted fairly well. I did well all through school, even graduating from high school early and in the top of my class. I always wanted to excel to prove that I was worthy and intelligent. I had to find something to feel good about myself. However, inside where no one could see, I was broken. I was entering the world feeling uncomfortable with my beauty, not feeling loved by my mother, father, or God. So tell me how far away was I really going to get from my past when my problems never were resolved? I was still a little girl looking for love, searching for the God I first met at age nine. This journey helped me to see the truth of who I had become and why.

Where It All Started

So I was at the end of this path and I was thinking, *God, now I understand why You brought me back to the past.* I thought I had forgiven when I left my past, but the only thing I had done was learn how to be silent in my pain. I walked out of my past, but I never really moved on. God showed me this was where it all started. This is important because God doesn't want you to keep living in your wilderness—learn the lesson, see Him, and get out.

It was during this time I felt like I had to do things to earn people's love because love was conditional. I had to keep my feelings inside so people wouldn't reject me. I also started thinking God's love was conditional too. I tried to make God human because of my own human experiences. I had forgotten about the experience I first had when God came to me at the age of nine. I hadn't done anything special. I just had a heart that wanted Him and He came in. His love was free, and I accepted it. His love was unconditional; that was the meaning He wanted me to have. But then after experiencing pain, love became twisted in my mind and even in my perception of God's love, which made it easy for me to become a part of a religion that taught me to prove my love through works for God.

Coming back here showed me what was really bothering me, what really had me bound. I can't say it enough, you can't forgive what you do not confess or know exists or has hurt you. You have to say what it is that has hurt you. You have to open your mouth and get it up out of your heart. When you suppress your pain, it will turn into anger; and if left unresolved, it will prevent you from forgiving. No matter how much time passes by, the images, thoughts, and emotions of your past are still with you because you have not gotten rid of them. You're arguing and getting mad at people today. But it's not them you should be confronting—it's someone from your past. You will never get loosed from your pain until you are willing to confront the truth of your past.

For so many years I thought I was only mad at my stepfather, but taking this journey helped me to see that I was even angrier with God and my mother. Who are you really mad at? I know it's hard to be this honest with your pain and possibly admit such intimate feelings toward a parent or the sovereign Creator of the universe, but holding it in is only keeping you trapped in your past. Confess it and let it go. The healing comes through confession not by being in denial.

I left my past still hurting and in anger because I never knew I needed to confess what happened there in order for me to leave my past. My mother really is a beautiful, loving and caring person. I was not able to get to know her as a young adult because of the perception I had of her as a child. I missed many years of getting to know how special a lady she really is. It is because she is committed and wants to believe the best of people that she didn't want to believe Terry did what he did. As a child, I didn't know about the "gray areas" and that she could hope for the best in Terry and still love me. I saw only things as black or white. This helps me to appreciate that God loved me despite my not understanding why He allowed my pain.

After that dark stormy night when my mother saw Terry in my room, I never thought about how it affected her. I had seen a naked, lying molester, but she had seen her husband, the stepfather and father of her children, her friend, partner, and lover. She was in shock. I can only imagine what she felt in seeing the reality of this scene unfold before her. I thought this was all about me as a child. But now that I'm an adult looking back, I realize we do not experience stories on an island by ourselves—there are many people involved with us all dealing with their hurts. The hurt doesn't just affect one—it always affects many, and it will become generational if it wasn't confessed in the past and was allowed to continue to cross blood lines. The blessing is even if it wasn't confessed in the past, it can be confessed now, and you can be made whole.

I wished someone had helped both me and my mom together because we both were hurt. Terry hurt us and we hurt each other. If we would have confessed the pain, we could have shared the pain in our hearts and healed, instead of allowing anger to twist the love we had for each other. For many years pain had created its own story in my life until the day I cried out to the Lord, and He showed me the truth of this journey. I allowed Him to put me back on the right path of light and love where anger and the enemy had no power over me anymore. In the absence of covered-up pain, the enemy can't use the weapon of anger against us, and then we don't have to be held captive to unforgiveness and bitterness.

So this was it. I thought the pain I shared that day when I stopped talking with God was because of the events leading up to my divorce. However, God allowed me to go back to remember that wasn't all of the story. I had to reconnect with my past to remember the same reasons many of the people who are stuck today were the same reasons for me too. It was our past. I had just forgotten where I had come from. We are defeated because of our thinking. We have to change the way we have allowed our past to define our God and the world around us. The enemy uses our anger to think like him and be used as a weapon against ourselves. I had to come back to remember what it takes to close the door to your past and live in your present.

You are going to have offenses every day of your life, but the purpose of this journey is to free you from your past so you can live in today, and not compound new offenses with the past. You need to know where you stopped devaluing you and made everyone else indebted to you. What hurt you? What shaped you? What hurt your heart so badly that you have since been controlled by anger and fear? Confess, confess, confess, and get free. This is where healing begins.

This is what I was trying to avoid. I thought I could tell people to forgive and ignore their pain, what hurt them, and why they have a lack of trust in God. Well, God showed me ironically using my own story to show how forgiveness doesn't start in the present; the journey begins with pain. After the confession of my pain to God, He helped me to trust Him with my heart again. When that happened, I was ready to obey and forgive. Come on—it's no time to slow down. We're moving through this wilderness.

~ 6 ~

Finding God's Love Again

It wasn't until I believed God was really with me that I fell in love with Him again. Belief and trust in God's love for you is essential before you are ready to cross over from your past into the present and begin walking in forgiveness. You can't really obey (from the heart) someone (even God) if you feel abandoned or hated by them in the wilderness. (See Deut. 1:26-27.) People keep telling you to forgive but you have to trust in the love of the one commanding you and assess your relationship with God. Forgiveness is a matter of the heart. When your heart is aligned with Gods,' then you can love others.

He knows the emptiness that you carry. Others may look at your life and think you have it all and are just selfish and immature because they can't understand how you can have so much and still complain about being unhappy. God knows that nothing is going to satisfy you because what you really need is the answer to the question: "God, why didn't You protect me?" before you will give Him back your heart. It's like being married and sleeping in different beds.

You don't know how to deal with these questions that tug at your heart. You don't want to experience what Job did when he expressed his doubt. So you ignore them and you get busy in works. You want God to know that you love Him, but you just don't trust Him with your heart.

Until God has your trust, He can't have your heart; and forgiveness is a matter of the heart. To forgive is an act of obedience and trust in God. I had it all wrong. I was trying to teach the class to get right with people; but I had forgotten that before I was ready to forgive, I had to first get right with God and trust in His love. Forgiveness begins with reconciliation between the hurting person and God. Once He has your heart, you will be able to forgive others. Thank God He is so merciful toward us while patiently waiting for us to find this truth in the journey. So how did God regain my trust?

Finding His Love

Let's go back to that day when I cried to Him and opened my heart, asking where He was. Then God said to me, "Remember that day?" I was thinking, "What day? There were a lot of days." He said again, "Remember that day?" I asked, "What day?" He said, "The day in the bathroom." My eyes almost popped out of my sockets. Yes, I knew what day He was talking about—that dreaded, awful, dark day when I thought it was the end. I never told anyone about that day and hadn't even thought about it, so He had to have been there.

I said, "Yes, I remember. What about it?" He said, "That was your last straw. You had had it with Stanley; you couldn't take any more. He was screaming and yelling uncontrollably. He had thrown glasses at you and cut you. He broke the television and punched a big hole in the wall. You thought for sure with all of that noise someone would call the police, but no one did. It was an unusually dark night. You could not remember a night being that dark except when you used to travel to the south when you were a little girl with your grandparents.

"Your husband was arguing all night. He went on and on ranting. The ranting got on your nerves more than anything. He wore you out. Just as the night was oddly dark, a dark thought came across your mind. 'No one cares—just end it. You have suffered enough. You have never been happy—just end it. Everyone will be better off.' So you walked right past him as if you or he were invisible and went into the bathroom. He began banging and banging on the door. You thought he was going to break it down. You sat on the toilet and couldn't cry any more. You didn't have the strength to cry. Somehow you had the strength to lift your arm up. I thought for a moment you were getting ready to pray to Me, but no, you just raised your arms to get a razor.

"Stanley was banging on the door until you got the razor in your hand, then a peace entered into your mind and the apartment that had never existed there before. All of a sudden the ranting, yelling, and screaming stopped. He didn't even try to pull at the door or ask you what you were doing. He wasn't threatening you to come out. It was as if someone had subdued his mouth and took away his power and voice. Remember, daughter?"

God now fully had my attention, and my heart. When He told me this information, He showed me He had been there with me. I couldn't believe this. God was telling me exactly what went on that night in my mind and in my heart, and only He could do that. He was there! I had forgotten about it.

God continued, "That peace was Me. I knew you couldn't take anymore, so I had to rush in. I know you don't think so, but I really do know just how much you can bear. The thing is when you picked up your cross to follow Me as a child; you wanted to share in My glory. You were too young for me to explain the suffering that came with it. I never told you about that because you weren't ready to carry it. The wilderness (pain) prepares you for the cross. And it is the wilderness that develops your character to test you so that I can trust you with My promises and share in My glory.

"I prepared you before you went into the wilderness. I sent you in with My love just like I did for My Son before I led Him into the wilderness and declared that He was My Beloved. If you knew your identity as My beloved, you too would have power. When the enemy tried to tempt you in the wilderness, you would be able to resist him, his temptations, offerings, and deception. You can't be defeated when you know who you are and that you are secure in My love. That's why I came to you when you were nine. What we experienced was real. I had sent Jesus to show you the way to endure the wilderness, but your anger and pain caused you to take your eyes off Me, and you lost your way.

"I was there in the bathroom, My child. You experienced the peace that surpassed all understanding, and there wasn't any explanation as to why it was happening. It was Me. I am Peace, and I gave My peace to you that night. I am a lot of things. I allowed you to go into the wilderness so that you will know I am your shield, banner, protector, comforter, and anything else you need. In that moment when your cross was too heavy, I came to carry it for you. I promised I would when you were a little girl, but you got lost. Think about it—what would stop a mad man like your husband in his tracks? It was Me, the great I AM. I came to your rescue."

The first time God told me this, my heart almost could not take it. I was filled with both joy and also remorse that I hadn't seen Him back then. I spent all those years thinking God didn't love me, when He did. I want you too to think about those times in your life when an escape was provided for you in the wilderness, a job came through, money came to you out of nowhere, an abusive husband left, an incidental finding at a routine medical visit was discovered that saved your life, a good Samaritan helped you when you were stranded, a friend called when you were having suicidal thoughts or just depressed, an invitation arrived to join a party when you felt all alone, that wayward child you haven't heard from in years all of a sudden returned home, a beautiful sunset was painted across the sky for you to appreciate—these are signs all around us to show us He is with us.

I remembered all of what He was saying. Yes, that night I was ready to end it. I had the razor to my wrist but I put it down and right then my husband suddenly stopped—not another knock, bang, curse, rant, nothing. I stayed in the bathroom all night and slept in the tub, and he left me alone. I didn't feel scared either that night for I was at peace. I had never before had a day of peace with him from the moment we were married. It was a miracle! When morning came, I said no more and made plans to separate from my husband. When he returned home I was gone, and I never lived with him again. It was what I first experienced that night that gave me the peace and courage to know I didn't have to live like that. Oh my God, He did provide my escape in more ways than I ever realized!

Yes, suddenly I saw my Daddy had rescued me. All those years what I wanted was for someone to protect me, subdue my enemy, and give me peace and security. And in the midnight hour, my God did it for me. Living in pain and anger can jack you up so much that even when God does show up, you still are blind. There was so much darkness around me and in my heart that I didn't even see the light when God had shone it mightily that night. I had to go back to see my past to realize that God had been there. Despite your darkness, if you look for it, there is light, but you have to be willing to see it. Let God take your heart back and lead you out of your darkness.

I found God's love again when I saw He loved me enough to be with me in my pain and help me. When you have been beaten emotionally, spiritually, and physically, it takes a little bit more convincing sometimes. I believed God was there, but I had still struggled a little with believing that He loved me unconditionally. If you think you can lose His love all the time, you never feel secure. I had to go back into my past to discover God's love for me, so I could show you His love for you.

Many people and religions don't want you to know about God's unconditional love because they fear this will give you a license to want to practice sin. So rather than tell the truth, they have tried to become God, making you subject to their religious views instead of allowing you to see the true, all powerful, merciful, unfathomable, unconditional, unfailing love of God that you need to get through the wilderness.

True love for God will make you not want to sin against Him, and because man and religion have kept this truth and prevented you from understanding His love, it is they who have contributed to a church full of weak, angry Christians. You have to hear the truth about God's love not just when it is convenient for religion. (When I say religion, I'm not speaking of those godly churches where Christ is the center and love is the mark of their identity and where disciples are made and shown how to have a relationship with God.)

Many of you including me continued to sin, because we never learned about the love of God that had the power to set us free from sinning. This is the same love that allows us to have salvation. God is love. It doesn't change. It says in Romans 8:35, "Who shall separate us from the love of Christ? Shall tribulation, or distress, or persecution, or famine, or nakedness, or peril, or sword?" There is never anything so great that can separate us from His love.

Because I had forgotten my own pain and where I had come from, I couldn't see the women's pain in the class. I was impatient with them. I wanted to hurry them along, ignore their pain, and just get to forgiveness. I wanted them to know that God loved them and for them to trust Him and obey Him right there on the spot, but they were still stuck. I didn't arrive there in one day, and yet I thought with a smile and a Bible I could lead them right out. I never want to forget again where I came from and what it took to get where I am today. I never want to be so insensitive or self-righteous ever again that I stop being a helper and become an accuser of someone's faith in their pain.

I had become offended by God and that anger caused me to question if He loved me. Some of the women in the class were offended too. Being offended by God opens our mind to a kind of reasoning that will cause us to get lost in the wilderness. We have to be honest about our anger toward God—that's the only way to get free.

Most of us have become offended by God (angry) because of our circumstances. Many of you may know the story of John the Baptist—he was the forerunner who prepared the way for Jesus. John baptized Jesus and saw the heavens open and heard God declare that Jesus was His "Beloved Son." He saw and heard of numerous miracles performed by Jesus. But when John was put in prison, he sent two of his disciples to ask Jesus if He was the Messiah. Pain (being in prison) caused him to take his mind off the true identity of Jesus for a moment because of his circumstances. When John became offended, he questioned not Jesus' love like I did but His very identity. Be honest with yourself, how have your circumstances caused you to become offended by God? What has it caused you to question about God—His love, wisdom, justice, power, or His very deity?

No doubt John was wondering that since Jesus did all of those miracles, had all this power, raised people from the dead, caused the blind to see, the lame to walk, the lepers to be cured, set demon possessed people free, He could easily get him out of prison if He wanted to. He couldn't understand why Jesus left him sitting there facing death.

John was listed in the elite company of limited people called, "There are none like them on the entire earth" category. Job, Moses, King David, and Abraham are a few mentioned in this club. However, when he experienced pain in his life, even John reacted the same way some of us have when we encountered pain because God didn't stop it or change our circumstances the way we thought He should. He became offended by Jesus. He could have chosen to remember all he had seen, experienced, and knew about Jesus. However, instead he allowed his pain to have more influence over his heart.

When God reminded me of the bathroom incident, I saw His love and power—it was my map out of the wilderness. I had to keep my eyes on Him and not allow my pain to cause me to become offended by Him. I regained my assurance that He was with me, and I decided to never again allow anything to cause me to question His love for me again (which in essence is to question His deity because He is Love [1 John 4:8]).

Accept who God says He is, not what you think, feel, or see through your circumstances. Allow Him to show you that He was there in your storms. Wait to see in His wisdom how He is using the evil done against you for your good (Rom. 8:28). Fall in love with God again because He never stopped loving you. When you are in love, you trust and you will obey. Would I forgive? Let's go and see…

~ 7 ~
Leaving My Past

After I had my experience with God, a weight was lifted off me. I had given the darkness, secrets, guilt, and shame in my heart to the Lord. When you let go and let God, you trust Him and give Him your pain, allowing Him to show you how to move on.

For the first time I had hope again. I wanted to actually live. There was a light in my heart that hadn't been there in years. I started to wake up anticipating the good in each day, and I went back to college, which was something I had always wanted to do. God and I had made many strides in our relationship, but I have to be honest I still was carrying some of that baggage from my religion in my mind. I believed God was with me and loved me, but I didn't know how to have a relationship with Him or feel secure in our love.

I knew God would work it out. Little did I know He was working it out already through one of my classmates. This classmate seemed happy all the time and was very energetic. Everybody wanted to be around him because he was so lively. He participated in all the discussions and kept it really interesting. I looked forward to seeing him in class, not to have a relationship with him, but just because he was a nice person.

One day he asked me why I looked so sad all the time. It's

funny, I didn't think I was giving off that signal, but I guess I was. There was something about him that felt safe, but I wasn't interested in letting him know me outside of class. I wasn't ready to let anyone get near my heart. However, after a few more weeks passed, he came up to me after class and said again that I was too pretty not to smile. I don't know why, but I opened up and explained why I was sad.

I told him I was so sad because I missed God. I wasn't sure if he even knew God. This was another God moment. God says, "If you seek you shall find, ask and it shall be given, knock and a door shall be opened" (Matt. 7:7). I went on to tell him that I used to attend an organization at least three times a week, conducting Bible studies, and engaging with others to share the gospel. God was a big part of my life then. I also told him how one day I gave all that up and now I felt so alone. My soul was thirsty for God, but I didn't want religion—I wanted something, deeper, stronger, more personal and tangible. I wanted something that no one could ever take from me. I wanted my own relationship with God.

This young man had no idea how long I had waited to share this with someone. It was by divine appointment we were together at this time in this place. He worked at a chemical plant and often had to take refresher courses in chemistry. He normally attended the downtown campus, but this particular quarter he wanted to try another one. He usually only took chemistry classes, but this quarter he wanted to take a class in business, and that's how we ended up being on the same path. Everything we go through is a part of our journey with God—nothing is wasted.

My classmate asked me what was stopping me from having a relationship with God if that was what I wanted. I told him that I didn't want to go back to being a part of a religion I was affiliated with. I told him they ingrained in me that only through them could you go to heaven or be saved.

I couldn't believe I was being this honest with him, but he was just easy to talk with. He showed me more concern in those few weeks than people had done who had known me all my life. He wanted to know what was in my heart. I told him I wanted to know that if I sinned, I could repent before God and didn't have to prove myself before a committee of men. I don't want anyone to determine the state of my relationship with God or the direction of my life. I wanted to know I could trust God when He says He forgives me and loves me and that He wouldn't take it back or banish me forever.

He just stared at me. He said he was saved, and the things he expressed about God were so sweet and pure, I could tell he had a real love relationship with God. He told me where he attended church, and I was surprised he had such assurance of God's love and spoke with authority in sharing his beliefs. His own beliefs were real—something that came out of his heart.

He was surprised that I was a part of a religion to which I had given so much control over my life. He respected me in class because I was one of the smartest people in it. So he couldn't understand how an intelligent person could become a part of a religion and not see the falsehood when a religion tries to determine whether or not you have repented or try to say who is saved. This was all foreign to him. What he didn't understand is that getting involved in false religions or bad relationships has nothing to do with intelligence. They are matters borne out of broken and deceived hearts.

We meet people all along the journey who will either help us or keep us captive in our journey. This man helped by catapulting me out of my past when he said that he knew he was going to heaven. He was a happy, joyful person with a light radiating out of him, just like I had when I was that little girl of nine and knew Jesus. How was he able to be so confident of his salvation? What did he know that I didn't know?

I asked him if he had a nickname because I never could remember to call him by his birth name. (It was an odd name.) He said his nickname was Magic. Now I thought this was a line, but it wasn't—that really was his nickname. He got it in high school because he was a good athlete and later went to college on a sports scholarship.

The more I talked with him, the more I saw him as Magic because he was bringing something back in my life I hadn't felt in a long time. He reminded me of a trust and a joy I once shared with God. He gave me hope again. If I could feel like he felt toward God, it would be magic. Magic didn't keep God up in heaven, far away and distant. He talked about Him in a personal, intimate way like a child who knows and loves their father. I had never seen a man have that kind of affection for God that was so genuine.

There was something about Magic—as I got to know him more, I saw Jesus in him with his love, peace, and joy. It was so refreshing to be around someone like this. In fact it seemed like the past had never affected him, and if it had, he showed it was his love and belief in God's love that had brought him through.

We had long conversations after class. I had always liked class before, but now I couldn't wait to get there. I was finally fellowshipping with someone who was helping me to get back on track with God. There was only so much we could talk about after class so he promised me he would bring me a book the following week.

The following week he brought me a book by an author named Charles Stanley, and it was about salvation. I devoured that book because it was so refreshing and simple to read. It helped me feel secure, learning about God's gifts of love and mercy. It clearly showed that His love wasn't predicated on my worthiness, efforts, or works.

What work of ours could measure up to being good enough to earn our salvation? What act could top Jesus' dying on the cross for us? If Jesus said He died once for all time, if He is the propitiatory sacrifice for our sins, then He paid the total price for our debt. What can we put in place of His blood to cover our sins if His death isn't enough? He promises us that His love will follow us, but we have to be willing to trust and seek Him.

I really was blessed by Ephesians 2:8-9, "For by grace are ye saved through faith; and that not of yourselves: it is the gift of God: Not of works, lest any man should boast." God showed me that there is nothing I could do, no work great enough for me to be saved. He wanted to give me the gift of salvation, and I could have it if I believed and had faith. He set it up that way so that no one could boast that they were good enough to earn their salvation. It has nothing to do with us and everything to do with God. The only part we play is whether or not we accept the invitation in faith.

I was starting to get excited as I pondered over the possibility that I could have eternal salvation. God told me He knew that I was having a problem trying to understand that He really loves me. He said that He gave His only Son to die for me so that I could have eternal life. This is real love. It wasn't that I loved Him first (1 John 4:9-10). He said He established the price and paid it with His Son's life (John 3:16) to prove His love.

To help me understand His love further, God reminded me about the story of Abraham and how he was willing to sacrifice his son Isaac to prove his love and faithfulness. God said, "When I saw that Abraham was going to do it, I stopped him out of My love for him and provided an animal sacrifice. Out of my love for him, I would not allow him to give up what was most beloved to him. But no one could stop Me when I had to offer my beloved Son. I gave Him up because I loved you, and the only way you could have eternal life was for Me to willingly offer the life of My Son."

I was starting to understand for the first time that what God did for me was out of love—it wasn't just a story in the Bible. It's easy for us to acknowledge the pain of a man who loses a child, but we sometimes fail to give God the same courtesy. It was time for me to appreciate what He did by accepting His gift.

As I reflected over God's sacrifice, He asked me, "Do you believe I sent Him? Do you believe He died for you?"

I said, "Yes Lord."

"Then why do you keep resisting My love when that is the reason why I sent Him? I AM LOVE, and I love you, My child."

It seemed too easy to believe I could be saved and I didn't have to do anything but have faith in Jesus, confess my sin, make Him Lord, and worship Him, and I could spend eternity with God (Rom. 10:8-10). The truth is that it is this simple. We may feel good, thinking we have attained a certain level of righteousness on our own, but this is false because without Christ there is no righteousness at all.

Do any of you struggle with the belief in eternal salvation? If you do, this may be why it's hard for you to accept God's forgiveness in your life or forgive others. It's hard to forgive when you still don't have the assurance of God's unconditional love in your own heart and believe you can lose it. In order to obey, you have to believe and be secure in His love for you.

I'm not trying to get into a debate on salvation because there are those who will tell you that you can lose your salvation. But let me say this to you—God's Word says if we can give good gifts being imperfect parents, how much more will He being perfect. I'm a mother and there is absolutely nothing my children can do to cause me to separate from them or never allow them to have a home. I can only feel this way because of the God in me. If we make God's love conditional like man's, we make Him human and take away His deity. He is the one who says His love is unfailing.

Just find God's love first and then study His Word for yourself. Trust God's Word and don't reason yourself out of what it says. You have to learn how to renew your mind by aligning your thoughts with God's and casting away any other thoughts that are contrary to what He says (2 Cor. 10:3-5). You have to find, believe, receive, and remain in God's love before you can forgive.

When the enemy tried to tempt Jesus in the wilderness, many people think the first temptation was centered on food because he was hungry, and the devil said, "Turn the stones into bread." But no, the first thing the devil said was, "*If you be the Son of God*, command these stones be made bread"

(Matt. 4:3 emphasis added). Did you catch that the enemy first said, "If you are the son?"

The enemy was attacking Jesus' identity and His knowledge of His Father's love. Was He secure enough in His Father's love that He would not have to try to tempt the Father to prove His love for Him? Isn't this what we do? Because of our circumstances in the wilderness, we say, "God, do this to prove You are my Father." And when He doesn't, we want His angels to catch us when we fall and get lost. Jesus entered the wilderness, led by the Holy Spirit, knowing who He was because God had just confirmed Him as His beloved Son.

The devil was trying to attack two things when he said, "If you are the Son." First the enemy left off the word "beloved." He never wants us to know we are loved, so he wasn't going to remind us by jarring our memory and calling us God's beloved. I allowed my circumstances to change who God had said I was before I went into my wilderness. Jesus came out of the wilderness full of power. Jesus knew He was subject to God, and He came to do His will. I had stipulations for God to prove His love, and when He didn't obey my will, I doubted His love and left my wilderness weakened.

When I started to feel His love and believe in it again, He became not just God but Father. He wanted me to comprehend two things. The first one is understanding humility. James 4:7-8 (NLT) says, "So humble yourselves before God. Resist the devil, and he will flee from you. Draw close to God and He will draw close to you." (I know I use this reference a lot but one of your keys to victory is surrender and that requires humility.)

I had to think about this a few times before I really

started to understand it. He was telling me to position myself where I was completely submitted to Him. That meant I should not allow any situation or person to cause me to believe something different than what I read in His Word. I had to be steadfast and single-minded toward Him and not allow fear to cause me to resist Him but resist anything that would separate me from His word and truth.

I was going to have to develop a mind-set where I wouldn't dare exalt my mind to question the sovereignty of God. I needed to trust Him so that His love would cover me at all times through the storms of life. In the wilderness, God was a cloud and pillar of fire for the Israelites: He was their guide, shield, and protection. As long as they trusted Him and stayed submitted to Him, they survived. I had to stop allowing my circumstances, anger, or pain to become bigger than my God and stay under His cloud to cover me.

I would no longer allow the devil's trickery, lies, and deception to draw me away from God. I would have to refuse to listen to anything he suggested. I would have to stand in God's love and have it perfected in me so that the enemy's voice became foreign to me, and I resisted him instead of God. Every time the enemy suggested God doesn't love me, I said God's truth is that He does and commanded the devil to flee.

When you get to this place of knowing God's love, there really is no choice but to walk in love. It is impossible to love God and not love His people, even those who have hurt you. When I'm not distracted by my pain, I'm not focused on me. I have confessed my anger, asked for forgiveness, and forgave, and that's how I can leave my past behind. And lastly, through the power of God's love, I never have to allow trials to separate me from God's love.

Before I show you how to forgive, I want to share something with you. I know you have been waiting to know if that guy who showed me what God's love looked like became my Magic in another way. Let me give you a resounding yes! We have been married for twenty-two wonderful years. He has never hit me, cursed me, betrayed me, been unfaithful to me, or done anything but love me. He was the first person other than God to really love me unconditionally even in my brokenness and fear. I have become who I am because of him since he led me back to Jesus. He listened to my pain and helped me find God's love. I wish I could write a whole book about this man, my "Magic." I still call him Magic, which is what most people call him too. They thought I gave him the name, but God gave him that name to let me know the gift, the miracle He was sending my way, after all the pain I had experienced. Magic brought restoration to my life. I love you, Magic, and I want the world to know it!

Together we both serve God with all our heart in the ministry. He is a minister and what I have said about him everyone who knows him agrees with too. It was out of love God brought us together. Magic is one of the most loving men God created. He is my friend, protector, lover, and a wonderful father to our children. He has a servant's heart—he serves our church, my extended family, and our friends. His love just keeps on giving. We have two beautiful daughters and two sons. Our girls will never have to marry a loser or be abused because they know what real love is. They have an earthly father named Magic who has shown them how to trust in their heavenly Father and in love. Our sons will be wonderful loving husbands because they have a role model to show them how to love their wife.

Today I know I am a child of God, redeemed, forgiven, saved by grace, delivered from the powers of darkness, strong in the Lord, blessed with all spiritual blessings, walking by faith and not by sight, transformed in my mind, more than a conqueror, and above all, loved by God. I am free and therefore I can love. When I was free from my pain, I knew what love was, and I was ready to walk in it.

Passing the Test

Before we got married, I encountered an unexpected person from my past. I left my downtown office one day to go out for lunch. As I was crossing the street, a man approached me who appeared to be homeless. He was dirty, and his clothes were torn and mismatched. His hair was filthy, long, and unmanaged. He started to approach me, asking loudly, "Can you spare some change?" As he came closer, I started walking faster past him and was getting ready to run.

I was afraid of the man so I did something that seems so strange to me now. I turned around and started to run back past him in the opposite direction to get away from him instead of keeping on ahead of him or crossing the street (another God moment). As I passed him, he called out my nickname. I had to stop because only a person who really knew me from the past would call me by this name. It is a name out of my childhood and I haven't used it or told it to anyone in my adult life. I had to stop even though I was afraid because this was someone who must have known me intimately.

I took another glance. Underneath all the dirt, the long disheveled hair, and the torn clothes, he still had that Christmas smile—it was my stepfather Terry. I went up to him and could not believe how old he looked. I felt sorry for him. After you begin walking in forgiveness, you will have compassion for the hurting because your pain is no longer your focus. My heart really hurt for him. I was so free in forgiveness that I had tears streaming down my face for him. The situation he was in showed me he had not escaped the demon inside of him. When you have Christ's love in you, you have more than enough to give to someone else who needs it, and in that moment he needed it. He asked me for some money to eat, but I invited him to eat lunch with me. McDonalds was nearby, so we just went there because I wasn't sure whether he was going to use the money on food or alcohol.

I didn't have any fear of him because in love, fear is cast out, and I was in God's love. (I'm not telling you to necessarily go eat with someone who has molested you. You have to use wisdom. I will discuss this further when I talk about how to reconcile. We definitely have to stop the madness of generational molestation and rapes by allowing our children to be around perpetrators. Don't leave your daughters and sons with abusers. The enemy is a deceiver and I don't want him to twist anything that I say and cause you harm by thinking I'm saying to live in some la-la land and go eat with your molester without discernment.)

It was day time, and I was downtown, and the streets were as crowded as sardines in a can. We were at a crowded McDonalds at lunchtime, so I was safe. Nonetheless, there was a peace in my heart—I had no fear, no anger, no pain, and no enjoyment out of seeing how he was. I was hurting for him but because I was in God's love, I knew that if I were in danger, I would have sensed it.

I have to admit, though, that I was surprised I did not have any anger in my heart at this man. As we sat across the table from each other, he stared at me, but it wasn't like the last time he was glaring at me. He said I looked nice and I believed him, and I didn't feel uncomfortable because it wasn't an inappropriate stare. He said I "looked so professional" and he was proud of me.

We did not talk about the past, except he wanted to know that the family was all right and that my mother was all right. He said he was sorry. I did not want to use manipulation or guilt over him; it was obvious that he was paying for his wrongs. I wanted to bless him. I didn't need to ask him all the "why" questions that I once thought I would if I ever saw him again. He couldn't give me any direction. It was obvious he hadn't found his own way. He had become seduced through sin into darkness through drugs. Satan doesn't care what door he uses to gain access into our lives just as long as we give him permission to enter.

Another reason I didn't have the desire to ask him all the why questions of the past—I didn't need for him to set me free. I didn't need an apology or revenge. I had learned the lesson from the wilderness—my power was in believing and holding on to God's love. His apology would set him free not me. I didn't need anything from him—I was free. When you cancel people's debts to you, it sets you free.

As I was leaving, I gave him a few dollars. He said he would pay me back. I did not believe him or know if I would ever see him again, but it didn't matter. I had it to give so I gave it; he needed it, and so he received it. The Bible says, "But if your enemy is hungry, feed him, and if he is thirsty, give him a drink for in doing you will heap burning coals on his head" (Rom. 12:20 NASB). True Christianity goes beyond just not seeking vengeance; it enables you to show benevolence. God wants us to draw our enemies to Him through the kind acts of our love.

Surprisingly a few months later my stepfather did come back to my job, and he paid me back and took me to McDonalds. After that, I never saw him again. A few years later I heard that he had died. In retrospect, I'm glad we had the opportunity to spend that time together, and I saw that I was no longer controlled by hate toward him.

I would like to think my showing the light and love of Christ toward him did something in him that day. He didn't look as broken when he came back to repay me. His desire to pay me back was a sign of his remorse in not wanting to take anything else away from me. Although this was a small act, it was something and I respected him for that. He didn't owe me anything. But in my canceling his debt, I allowed him to walk in his freedom too.

I hope my stepfather found Christ before he died. I don't wish anyone to go to eternal hell. I was able to share my heart by not destroying his broken heart when I saw it needed some mending. I didn't know how to start up a conversation about salvation with him at the time, but I did show him the love of Christ. Hopefully he saw that if I could forgive him, then God could too; and if he heard God calling him, he drew near to God before he died.

It's okay if you are not here yet. Just keep following me through the journey. I'm not judging you; I was there. It wasn't always easy for me, but when you begin to walk in forgiveness it does become easier.

This was it. This was what it really took before I was

ready to forgive. I'm not saying I want you to take months or years; no, God forbid that. Nevertheless, on the journey I saw it did take more than a few scriptures to deliver me. It took being reconciled with God and love before I could walk in love and forgive. We're out of the past; let's move on.

~ 8 ~
Counterfeit Forgiveness

For you who believe that you can never be happy or free from your past, I want you to see that is a lie. You have the power to leave your past behind if you will follow these steps. There isn't one perfect roadmap to make your journey but use this to make the start. I had learned the secret was to just be honest about my pain, give it to God, accept God's love, and choose to walk in it. I thought I had learned everything I needed to know about forgiveness. Who would have thought that the enemy could deceive me here when I was walking in the light but he did. The Bible says he disguises himself as an angel of light (2 Cor.11:14).

I want to talk about what it means to forgive, but first I want to help you be able to recognize genuine forgiveness from the counterfeit kind. It makes a difference in being able to stay free and attain the fruit and blessings that only comes from walking in real forgiveness.

The enemy doesn't care what you believe you are doing just as long as it keeps you from doing what God wants. He knows once you're walking in love, he can't deceive a true Christian into thinking that it is okay not to forgive; we know God's Word clearly says otherwise. On the other hand, if he can deceive us into thinking we have forgiven when we haven't, he still gets what he wants—an angry heart that will eventually cause us to separate from God.

The enemy was brilliant, allowing me to think I had forgiven everyone in my past when I hadn't. As long as I thought I was pleasing God, I wouldn't think I needed to change. However, when seeds of unforgiveness began to surface, God showed me there was a problem. I wasn't enjoying that presence with God I had grown accustomed to. There was a distance. I was secure in His love and my salvation, so it wasn't anything like that. But there was dryness. And then God let me know where there is unforgiveness, you are not welcomed at His altar, and He doesn't want your gifts. You must go and make it right. I couldn't imagine who I needed to forgive, because everything seemed so right.

Life was really good. I had everything I ever wanted. I finished college and became a registered nurse. I got certified as a lay Christian counselor, and I had a loving husband and family. I had started getting to know my father and my mother and I was becoming closer and closer every day.

I thought since I was more mature, knowledgeable, and had such an understanding of forgiveness that I wouldn't get stuck in the past anymore. I didn't think I had to practice those simple steps of confessing my pain and anger, remembering God's love, and walking in forgiveness. Confronting pain to prevent darkness and anger from taking anchor into your soul has to become a lifestyle. I thought I had only needed to do this with the hard stuff from the past and that was over now. I thought that since I had forgiven my stepfather, God, and my mother, I didn't have to keep doing it. Confession makes you aware of what's hurting you that's why it's easier to deny your pain in silence. Confession starts your healing, but it's a continual process. Thinking I didn't have anything left to confess gave me a false sense that I had forgiven all of my past when I hadn't. I was set up to walk in counterfeit forgiveness because I was still carrying unresolved pain. This also caused me to give the enemy access into my present again, and I hurt someone I really loved.

What is counterfeit forgiveness? Let me share another part of my shoes to explain what it looks like instead of trying to define it. I told you my biological father wasn't around a lot when I was a child, but I had always hoped he would allow me to have a place in his life. I had just accepted that he would never love me. I never knew why he and my mother didn't make it. In fact I didn't know much about him, but his mother and sister and brother stayed connected to me. There's a reason why I'm bringing this up. When I became an adult I saw him on several occasions, and he even attended my first wedding and gave me away at my second wedding. I never thought I was angry at him because he wasn't around enough for him to impact my life, or so I thought. After having gone through the journey, I did learn that he meant more to me than I had realized. I wanted his love so much as a child. However, now that I was an adult, I thought all of this was behind me.

He was married and had another daughter who is seven years younger than I am, but she didn't know she had a sister. Although he attended my wedding, we still were not as close as I wanted to be in his life. I didn't feel like I was his daughter so it was okay that I didn't call him Dad. He lived in the same city as I did, but I wasn't invited to visit his home until years after Magic and I had married.

Anyway, I had never imagined that I would ever have a

relationship with my sister. However, because of complications after having our second daughter, I had to be hospitalized for three weeks because I was seriously ill. It was then that my father finally revealed to my sister who I was because he didn't know if I was going to make it. I was twenty-eight and she was just finishing undergraduate school.

She called me in the hospital and I couldn't believe it. I thought surely I was going to die for this to happen. I was very happy to hear from her. We said we would get to know each other when I got better. She didn't know that she was a little inspiration for me to get better. There are no words to express what the thought of having my sister in my life finally meant to me. I had never imagined that my father would bring us together and it was happening.

I was no longer a kept secret. At that point I felt that my father really was beginning to love me, and I was so thankful that he was there with me. My sister and I decided we were going to get to know each and not let anyone prevent us from having a relationship if we wanted one. If our relationship failed, it was going to be because of us.

She told me we were going to take it slow and just get to know each other first. After I was released from the hospital, she came to see me. We hit it off instantly, and I loved her and she loved me. We finished each other's sentences, liked the same music, and had a lot of the same ideologies. I had always wanted a sister like that. I had sisters growing up, but there was always jealousy and strife among us. I never knew why, but my sisters never really allowed me to share their world. We loved each other but just didn't show it in a way that each other felt it. Maybe that's a result of pain—people who don't know how to love.

Our first meeting wasn't awkward at all. There was no anger, pain, or jealousy in the room. We just talked and talked and talked. Oh, I loved my sister! We became good friends, and she adored our girls. At the time Janay was three and Megan was a baby. Summer, my sister, was excited to be an aunt. I was her only sibling, so this was the only way for her to be an aunt. She would get Janay on the weekends and take her to visit her college campus. They had a ball.

Things were great. I had never thought I would really know my father, and then I even got to know my sister too! I had everything I wanted. My sister and I often talked a lot. She allowed me to share in her life during this season, and I was happy. I didn't worry about what we had missed. I talked with her about dating and about God, encouraging her when school was overwhelming. I just loved my sister. I watched her graduate and go on to medical school and become a Doctor of Medicine. I was so proud of her.

When Summer and I developed our relationship, we never talked about the fact that we had been kept separated from each other. I never shared my story with her. I made her think everything was over. I was healed and all was forgiven. In fact I never even wanted her to know I had experienced any real pain, molestation, or physical abuse in my family, abuse from my first husband, or mental anguish from the religious organization. No, I just wanted her to think I was this strong Christian and a loving big sister. I was free from my past. I didn't want to bring the darkness back up. I forgot that what you don't confess isn't over. Pain doesn't die; it just lays dormant until anger grows, takes root, and the enemy uses it against you to attack. I should have known this, but I had forgotten what I had learned in the wilderness. (Actually it

110

was revealed to me about Counterfeit Forgiveness when I had first started teaching classes on forgiveness. How about that for confidence when God is convicting you while you're teaching?)

I didn't realize that because I had only confessed my anger about my stepfather, mother, and God, I had dealt with only half my past. I never thought about the fact that my father rejected me most of my life, and he took care of this beautiful young lady, my sister, and helped her on her way to become a doctor but did nothing for me. I thought if I said I forgave it, and it was behind me, I was done. That's deception, and this is how you walk in counterfeit forgiveness. Just because you display acts of kindness doesn't mean your heart is right; it doesn't mean you are really walking in forgiveness. You can't forgive what you don't confess; if you don't remember anything else, please remember that.

I hate to have to mention this about my father because he is truly one of the sweetest men you can ever know. He is faithful and committed to his family. I'm thankful that he is my father and I am not making excuses for him. He did reject, abandon, and forsake me. But that was in the past. I made it through the wilderness to the other side of forgiveness and saw that one season doesn't make the totality of a person. This goes for the person hurting and the one who caused it. Who he is today far outweighs who he was back then, and I wouldn't understand this journey if God didn't allow for his heart to be hardened toward me for a season. However, true to God's Word, He did use it all for the good. (In the last chapter you will read a poem my father wrote me, thanking me for my love.)

I know it will be difficult at times for my father to read

this, and this is one reason why I was reluctant to write this book. But there was no other way to write it without including this story. My father regretted what he did. Even to this day, he brings up guilt, but because of my love I cover him, and in God's grace, He covers us both. The past is over. We were experiencing a wonderful relationship, but because I didn't admit the pain that was in my heart because of my father's rejection, the enemy waited until he had an opportunity to use anger against me (1 Pet. 5:8). The enemy is a deceiver who hides behind darkness. I didn't know there was any pain left because I wasn't feeling angry anymore. Anger usually is the gauge that shows us what's in our heart. Things were going great. This is how the enemy deceives you. If something hurts you, it's still there. Pain doesn't die—it doesn't matter how long ago it happened. My father had hurt me in my past, and I had never confessed it. I thought I had just moved on. If you don't confess it, when an opportune time arises, the enemy is going to use it against you. That's why no matter how you try to forget, certain memories still come back to haunt you. God is trying to let you know hurt is still in your heart so you can confess it, not deny it, and get free. So what happened?

For years Summer and I had the best of times together. My girls and I would visit her and stay with her while she was away at medical school. We were so proud of her. Time went by and we still never talked about the fact we came into each other's lives when we were adults. She tried a few times to voice her anger saying she couldn't believe "Daddy was preaching moral values to her and he had a baby and never was a father to me."

She was mad at Daddy, but for some reason it made me

angry whenever she made those comments. God was trying to open the door to allow the light in, sending me clues, but I kept reminding myself that I was so righteous. So I guess in my pride the enemy was allowed to deceive me. I was worried how I would look if Summer heard my story.

I was the big sister, talking about power and the love of God, and encouraging forgiveness, I didn't want to look like I hadn't forgiven by bringing up the past. The deception was holding the pain of the past in, thinking I could live a blessed life and not become stuck. I had taken the journey to know the truth, but because I wasn't operating in God's love (instead of fear), I worried if I confessed how I really felt, that I would lose her and my father. When I started operating in my own love, I started becoming weak again.

When Summer graduated from medical school, we had become so close that she even dedicated a portion of her speech to me during her ceremony. She attributed my love, strength, faith, and encouragement as inspiration for those hard times when she wanted to give up. I could not believe I had impacted her life like that. I was so proud of her, and I was honored to be a part of her life. She had a whole slide show of pictures of us—she had captured us together in such a short amount of time to tell a beautiful story that showed our love and friendship. However, it was all about to change.

The problem was I still had pain in my heart and because I didn't confess it, it became anger. In counterfeit forgiveness, for a while everything looks good on the surface. It looks like you have forgiveness and I had fruit—our love.

After she received her doctorate certificate for medicine, I started having thoughts that I had not had in the six years we had been in each other's life. I had thoughts like *Why didn't I have a chance to go to college? Why couldn't my father love me enough to be there for me too?* They lived in beautiful homes; Summer had the best education and was exposed to the arts. She spoke so well that she could socialize with the elites in society.

Those thoughts were warnings that I still had some hidden darkness in my heart. Since I thought I had arrived already in a place of forgiveness, when God was trying to send me these signs, I denied them. I didn't let His light shine on my heart and reveal the counterfeit just as when a light is shown against a fake dollar bill and exposes it. If I would have confessed my hurt and anger and given it to God, the truth would have been identified and I would have been set free. Forgiveness can't take place in denial. This allowed the enemy to have a foothold in my life again.

Because I was ignoring the light, I started to act in darkness. Sometimes my sister would make comments about our father that would make me mad. I felt like it was so selfish for her to talk about him the way she did when he had done so much for her. My father and I started getting very close. We started sharing holidays and celebrations together, and he would come to the girls' dance and piano recitals. He would not miss any events in their lives. For the first time, I felt like I was really a part of my father's life and his family. I felt like I was his daughter too.

As my relationship continued to grow with my father, my sister would make comments to me like, "Whenever you call, Daddy comes running to you." I thought, *Really, I just had him for a few years, and he's trying to spent time with me and my family, give us love, and you're jealous?* I'm thinking this but I never said anything to her. I just smiled and acted like those words didn't hurt me. I didn't want to seem immature or ungodly so I dismissed the feelings of anger I was experiencing toward her.

She made comments that she felt like Father was giving me more attention than her. For the first time he was showing me the love I had always yearned from him, and she was trying to make me feel guilty. But I never told her how I felt. I didn't realize how threatened she was. Neither one of us were willing to see the other's pain.

It never occurred to me that it was natural for her to be jealous or threatened about seeing her father become so attached to another person, even if I was her sister and his daughter too. Up until this point she never had to share his affection with another sibling. It never occurred to me that I didn't know if she was ever happy in her big pretty home. It is crazy to think that we just walked into each other's life and never discussed the past. I needed to confront my past and clean it out so I could continue to live in my present, blessed life.

All of a sudden I began forgetting about all that I did have. I was forgetting about the blessings in my present—my husband, my family, and how I had gone back to college to become a registered nurse. I was blessed. I didn't want to tell my sister that her comments were offending me and ask what was wrong with Dad spending time with me and my girls. Fear kept me from sharing my true feelings because I didn't want to lose her. However, remember when you are operating in counterfeit forgiveness, the gifts that come from it are only short lived. Just like when counterfeit money is discovered, the purchases have to be returned. If you don't recognize the problem, confess your pain, get free, walk in God's love, and

forgive, you will lose it all anyway. The love we were culti-
vating was in jeopardy because it was being purchased with
counterfeit forgiveness.

Counterfeit Unveiled

It was never more evident that the seed of unforgiveness
was growing in my heart than when my sister asked me to do
something that was very important to her. After she became a
doctor she met a wonderful young man and they fell in love.
When he asked her to marry him, she asked me to be in her
wedding as matron of honor. I made up some excuse why I
had to decline. Not only was I not in her wedding, I didn't
give her a wedding shower or participate with the friend who
graciously gave her one. I can't believe I did that to her; she
honored me, and I rejected her.

I was so wrapped up in my own feelings that I became
lost in the wilderness again and before I realized what was
going on, my relationship with her was falling apart. All of a
sudden I was consumed with jealousy and anger. I didn't understand it. I loved her and never wanted to hurt her. I felt
intimidated to be in her wedding because many of the people
in her party were doctors and I was feeling self-conscious. I
also had been struggling with my weight for many years, and
I didn't have the confidence to be with all those beautiful
bridesmaids.

If I had remained focused on God's love, I would have remembered where real beauty comes from, and I would not
have been struggling with self-image problems. Being in a
place of darkness, I was listening to lies about my beauty,
confidence, intelligence, and self-worth. I became a punching
bag for the enemy to accuse me and deflate my ego. I had

given him a foothold into my life again through unconfessed anger.

I did attend her wedding but after that, our relationship suffered and really has never been the same. I have regretted not being in her wedding every day since. I wished I could take it all back and start over again. After this, my relationship with Summer was almost non-existent. I had just about destroyed the blessing I had always said I wanted.

Whenever we would talk, it was now very superficial. She couldn't trust me with her heart. She always acted cordial toward me, but she kept me at a distance. She never told me how much I hurt her. As usual we just ignored the past and thought we could move on. This is why so many of our relationships are suffering today. We need to share the pain behind each other's anger to get free.

A key to knowing if the forgiveness is real is if you still have bad thoughts from the past that bring you pain. Where there is pain, there is anger; and where there is anger, there is unforgiveness. Just because you display righteous external behaviors doesn't mean you have forgiven. Forgiveness is a matter of the heart and what is in the heart will eventually come out.

Because she wasn't honest about the pain I had caused her, she too was walking in counterfeit forgiveness. Years have passed and our relationship is still fragile. It's ironic that just a few days ago while re-editing this chapter, I was cleaning my bedroom and came across some pictures of my sister's wedding ceremony. Once again I realized how I had lost out on some important memories and experiences that God was trying to give me. Her wedding would have been the first really significant thing we would have shared in each other's life. God had given me an opportunity for restoration, giving me back what the enemy took from us, but because I was stuck, I missed a beautiful moment. Looking at these pictures brought such sadness in my heart as I saw what the enemy had stolen from us.

The Bible says not to be hearers of the word but doers, lest you be deceived (James 1:21-23). Counterfeit forgiveness is being deceived in your thinking that you are being obedient to God's Word and walking in love, mercy, grace, and righteousness when in reality you're walking in darkness. As Christians we are no longer supposed to be thinking of ourselves more than others, but we are to put the needs of others before our own, even if they have hurt us (Romans 12:3). There was no reason why I should not have accepted her invitation and the honor to be in her wedding except that my heart was in darkness and I refused to acknowledge it.

I think we underestimate how much power the enemy has over us when we walk in darkness. The Bible says in anger he has a mighty foothold in our lives. I didn't want to feel that way toward my sister, but it was like I had no control. I was becoming another person. It wasn't like I was thinking I wanted to hurt her and make her pay for what my father did to me. The thoughts were not even mine. Just because you think something doesn't mean the thought belongs to you. But without confessing your anger, the enemy stays attached to you and deceives you into thinking his thoughts are yours. He gets you to agree with him. We have to stay humble before God and resist the devil so he will flee from us.

After writing this chapter, the Lord placed it on my heart to confess to my sister my feelings of hurt from our past, how her statements affected me about complaining about our father, and apologize for hurting her. It wasn't about me or her, or trying to justify my own viewpoint. It was about being honest with each other so that we could begin to really heal our relationship and get free from the past. It was about shedding the light on the situation so that the enemy could be cast out of our minds and hearts (2 Cor. 10:3-5). It was time for us to stop agreeing with the enemy. We were not each other's enemy. God is love and in love we could get through this.

It was hard at first for me to confess my feelings and apologize. I tried to reason that too many years had gone by and I didn't want to open up Pandora's Box. I thought maybe she was over it, and I would be jeopardizing our relationship even more. I was a leader now, being used in the ministry, and had even started writing this book. I knew that obedience was better than sacrifice (1 Samuel 15:22), and yet I was still trying to negotiate with God. He doesn't want our acts of service; He wants a yielded, surrendered, and obedient heart.

So I humbled myself. I called my sister and apologized for the pain I had caused her. I confessed my jealousy of our father taking care of her and not being there for me. I confessed how she made me mad by complaining about him or about the time he spent with me and my girls. She accepted my apology and our relationship is now in a place where it can begin growing again. Until you deal with your pain, it will continue to hurt you and everyone that comes into your life.

The wonderful thing about this book is I know it works because I have the fruit in my life as evidence and I have seen it bless so many. Eventually I had to have a talk with my father too. Today I have a wonderful relationship with my father and mother. The relationship between my sister and me still isn't what it used to be when we first became connected. I don't know if she is free, she never confessed her pain from us being separated as children, or what I did to her, or even what she did to me. But I believe God can bring us closer together.

If pain is left unconfessed, the enemy can use deception to make us think everything is fine so that we will not make the changes that need to be made in our hearts to really operate in God's love and not our own. I'm not just talking about my sister and me, I'm talking to anyone reading this who has not spoken to a family member, or friend, refuses invitations, or just prefers to text rather than call. If unforgiveness is not the problem, what is preventing you from walking in God's love?

I am whole and healed and walking in God's love today. I have forgiven those who hurt me, and I've forgiven myself for hurting others. As you continue your journey, confess your pain and anger and get free, walk in God's love and forgive, don't allow anyone to pull you back into the wilderness because of guilt, shame, and condemnation. If you have confessed your sin to God, you are forgiven (1 John.1:8-9). If you have tried to apologize and it isn't accepted, keep pressing through into the journey.

This isn't to say don't think about those you have hurt. Try to make it work; go apologize whether you did wrong or not. Be sensitive to their heart. Give them an apology that reaches their heart and goes beyond their ears. That means coming with more than the words "I'm sorry." Let them know why you're sorry. Too many people don't know how to apologize, and while you may leave thinking you accomplished something, the person is still hurting. We must pray continually that one day we all will walk in the freedom of God's love. After you have done all that you can, all that God asked you, move forward.

What did God ask? He said when there is strife and anger in relationships to lay down your gifts at the altar and go make it right. (It may take several times.) Relationships are what matters most with God, not the singing, praising, shouting, even the worship. After you have done what you were told, step aside, because more than likely when another Christian can't receive an apology from a sister, a brother, father, mother, or friend, the person they really have the problem with isn't really you anyway. They need to take this journey to see what really has them bound.

We keep acting like we can't forgive anyone when we've been hurt, but we have hurt others too. God wants us all to forgive because "all have fallen short of his glory" (Rom. 3:23). There is no perfect person reading this book, but there are many who are bound. If you want to get free, you are going to have to forgive. It is God and Him alone who rescued me because I found His love, grabbed a hold of it, and followed it. The enemy doesn't want you to forgive because he wants to keep you stuck, but the first person to get blessed will be you.

We all struggle with forgiveness and try to justify our reasons for disobedience to God. Counterfeit forgiveness can keep you from experiencing all that God wants for you and to lose what you have received already. I learned that a person doesn't have to be in your life for you to be angry at them. It doesn't matter if the person is alive, dead, or absent, pain is pain and until you reconcile with it, you will not be able to move on. It didn't matter that my father wasn't there physically; he still hurt me and I had never confessed it.

God wants you to acknowledge that their absence has hurt you and be honest about what you missed out on and how it affected you. Until you do this, you will continue to be that angry kid on the inside with twisted thoughts. Confess it; get it out so that you can heal. No one has to understand but you and God. God has shown you how to be honest with your pain, so do it. Take your own journey. Get the hurt out so that it can stop hurting you and everyone around you.

Summer paid the price for the anger I still had toward my father. I never really told him how I felt. I kept it bottled up. My mother suffered—life was hard for us. I should have talked to him, but I was afraid because I didn't want to lose him, or just give it to God the way I had learned. I didn't need necessarily to confess my pain to a person to be free. I had never confessed my anger to my mother or stepfather and I was free. The important thing was that I just had to confess it, first to God; and if He wanted me to confess it to my father later, then I would. You don't need the person to be present to make your confession. Otherwise, many of you would never get free especially for those whose parent, spouse, or the person who hurt you is deceased. No one has to stay stuck; this is the beautiful thing about this journey. Just give it to God.

I never confessed that I was jealous of my sister. It wasn't her fault that she grew up with two parents and was well taken care of and able to fulfill her dreams and become a doctor. If I would have confessed my jealousy quickly and done the righteous thing instead of professed righteousness, God could have cleansed my heart (1 John 1:8-9).

Nevertheless, I had to learn this experience of counterfeit forgiveness. God is using my life to show you my shoes so you too will recognize real forgiveness.

If you still have any negative feelings about the past that are not in harmony with God's Word, don't be so quick to deny that you have unfinished business. Surrender to the leading of God when He is trying to speak to you. When you still have feelings of hurt and don't understand why, I suggest that you pray Psalms 139:23-24, "Search me O Lord and know my heart; test me and know my thoughts. Point out anything in me that offend you, and lead me along the path of everlasting life." I had to do more than read these words— I had to surrender to them.

Counterfeit forgiveness is even more serious than unforgiveness because it causes you to have a false sense of arrival and no need to change or improve. You will not change something if you don't believe there is a problem, so the enemy has you right where he wants you. One clue that unforgiveness is still lurking around you is that you have feelings of fear, pain, hurt, or low self-esteem about yourself. When you're being led more by emotions rather than by the spirit of God, check your heart. Sometimes when there is a standstill in your relationships, unforgiveness is the obstacle and results in unanswered prayers and blessings. You have to wait at the altar until you have made your relationships right or at least tried to do so. It doesn't mean you can't come to God until the relationship is fixed, but you have to have tried with love in your heart.

We can render the enemy powerless if we stop living in anger and denying it. We can render the enemy powerless if we humble ourselves and submit to God's love and forgive.

There is hope no matter what side of the journey you are on if you allow God to take the lead and reveal what's really in your heart. Now we will talk about forgiveness...

~ 9 ~

Stepping Into Forgiveness

When I first started teaching forgiveness, I wanted to start right here—at the end of the journey. I didn't want anyone to know my story, and I thought it was harmful to have people bring up their past. Never did I imagine that there in the past is where healing began. Now when I look back, I wonder about how anyone can ignore a person's heart and try to convince them that they have the answer to help them. It seems so unbelievable. My story was the light to expose the darkness and open the heart for us to come together. After the barriers are exposed and the light shown, the heart is prepared to receive the message of forgiveness. The enemy will send messages, thoughts, and memories to distract or try to get you angry, but you are free. Speak the truth, draw near to God, and the enemy will flee.

Now I can tell you forgiveness is really about keeping you free. Confessing your pain releases all the poison—the secrets, guilt, shame, bitterness, anger, fear—all that was stored up and destroying you on the inside and not just the events of the past. Confession loosens your heart and prepares it, but forgiveness sustains the heart. It keeps you walking in love and in the light, and keeps the enemy away.

Forgiveness begins with a choice, but it must become a lifestyle as you mediate on the goodness of God and His love, walk in thanksgiving, and apply the word of God in your life. This lifestyle will help you do what seems so contrary within your soul—forgive.

When I was young, if someone would have told me one day I would see my stepfather again and I was going to feel better if I forgave him, I would not have believed it. If someone would have told me that I would have felt blessed when I fed him at the restaurant that day, I would have thought they could only say that because they had not walked in my shoes. But the truth is, I was blessed when I blessed him. So now that I have shared *My Shoes,* you can see that I understand why it's hard to forgive, and why you find it hard to believe a person who experienced pain would tell someone to forgive. Now that I have shared my story, will you walk in my shoes and forgive and see that God is faithful and His word will truly bless you? Keep sharing and helping others learn how to get free.

We want to understand why we should do something—the logic in the command—and He doesn't ask us to understand; He asks us to obey. Are you ready to obey?

Just keep telling yourself that you want to be blessed and be able to stop feeling pain when you think about the past. If you want to receive God's promises and enter into His rest, you must trust Him. Trusting in God is not based on feelings or human knowledge—it is based on faith (Heb. 11:1). God has given us all a measure of faith to apply His will in our life (Rom. 12:3). I'm praying that you will use your faith to help you walk in the light of God's Word.

In this chapter I will discuss some misconceptions about what it means to forgive. And discuss practical ways to apply God's principles in your life and make forgiving a life style. Forgiveness is so abstract that again I wanted to apply it to everyday experiences to help you see the real picture: Here are some areas we'll discuss:

Forgiveness...
Chooses not to keep records
Chooses to forget
Chooses not to avenge
Chooses not to gossip
Chooses to be merciful
Chooses to be gracious
Is a matter of the heart
Helps your offender with their guilt
Doesn't need an apology
Does not welcome bitterness
Forgives God
Unforgiveness is idolatry

Chooses Not to Keep Records

Once you've confessed your pain, you have to keep your heart clean by not continuing to bring the hurts back up. After you let it go, don't file it away so you can bring it up again. This means you don't bring the offense up every time you become angry. You don't want to keep a file cabinet to store hurts of the past and of today because this keeps you stuck or just prevents you from progressing in your relationships or life the way God wants for you.

It is important to bring up your pain. However there is a

way to bring it up that is for really helping you to move forward and not just to blame others. If you are working through your pain, you can select a godly, mature person to walk you through, but whenever you just want to bring up the past to anyone that isn't to help you, it's a trap. A lot of your confession needs to start with God, because He is the one to show you what's in your heart so you don't have to keep bringing up things rehearsing the bad every time something comes across your mind. Pray and see how God wants you to resolve it once he reveals the hurt. But remember, people can't heal or free you. You are confessing your pain from preventing poison to continue to grow in your heart and allowing anger to be used as a weapon against you.

You have to learn how to share your pain in a healthy way—one that doesn't hold hostage either you or the person about whom you're talking. There is a kind of regurgitation of the past that is not for closure or healing. The memories will serve only as an anchor to hold you captive in your mind and be a mirror of your pain. In this unhealthy way, you want everyone to get mad at the one who caused you pain, and you're not seeking a listening ear or godly advice. When you bring up your pain, you will have to resist taking back the thoughts to stay angry after you have given them to the Lord. It's not denying what has happened but rather choosing to put it behind you. Psalms 103:12 says, "As far as the East is from the West, so far hath he removed our transgressions from us."

There is a difference in bringing up your past for your good or for harm. I'll give you an illustration. Imagine you are invited to a singles' event at your friend's church. Without your knowing, your ex-finance, who cheated on you with your best friend, attends that church, and you see him there. Another friend, who invited you, knew nothing about the situation, and she thinks very highly of your ex-finance. In fact, he is the minister of the singles' ministry. If you bring up the records to your friend of what he did to you, you are just using your past to hurt your ex-finance. When deciding when to bring your past up to others: Ask yourself if telling your friend about your past will help either you or them today.

Maybe your friend was introduced to the Lord through your ex-finance. Maybe her faith is not strong enough to hear about another bad thing that a Christian has done to someone. Maybe your ex-finance has really changed, and now he is using his experiences to help other single Christians. Remember, out of our mess comes the most powerful messages and testimonies to help others. How would going to a Christian event and bringing up your past be for the good? What is your motive? Is it for light or darkness? In this situation, bringing up the past would not help anyone.

On the other hand, if when you were confronted with the situation of seeing your ex-finance, and later you discussed it with your friend, is it possible to bring up the past so that it could be used for good? Yes. The difference is your motive in bringing up the past. You could tell your friend that you were not able to stay at the event because there was someone there (without naming names) that you did not want to see from your past. You could tell your friend that you are struggling with a painful breakup and that it's still affecting you today. This is being honest about your pain. It's not shared for spite or vengeance. However, you should only bring your pain up to someone you feel is spiritually mature and healthy themselves before discussing your past. Otherwise it could turn into a male bashing or pity-party. If your motives are sincere and you really want a breakthrough from your past, you will be humble enough to receive the word of God when your friend walks you in forgiveness. So in this case bringing up the records was to move on not stay stuck.

Chooses to Forget

I have always heard "to forgive means to forget." And people have said they couldn't forgive because they couldn't forget. The devil is just a deceiver; he even has us repeating his lies. This is not biblical. However, in the Bible, God illustrates that in forgiving us, He chooses not to remember our wrongs or bring them up. It doesn't mean He can't remember because it has been erased out of His mind. And it doesn't mean that we have to deny what happened. God is a spirit, and we must worship Him in "spirit and truth."

It's almost impossible to forget unless something so traumatic has happened, and your body is allowing you not to remember for your healing. Usually, in those cases where you can't remember, this is an unconscious act of forgetfulness. However, to forgive is a conscious act. God wants us to willingly obey His Word by forgiving.

Chooses Not to Avenge

We must give up the desire to punish others. It is natural to want to see people get what we feel they should for hurting us. However, vengeance belongs to the Lord. Deuteronomy 32:35 tells us that vengeance and recompense belong to God. He won't work it out for us if we are in the middle, trying to do our own thing. We have to trust in God and leave it to Him to bring about justice.

I didn't have to do anything to harm my stepfather. I don't know what happened in his life after that day when my mom threw him out. It was obvious that life was hard. When I saw him that day on the street, wrinkles lined his face; sores on his knuckles showed through his gloves without the fingers; dirty, torn clothes covered him; and his teeth were protruding from his mouth. He once was a handsome, strong, loving man. That day he looked thirty years older than he was. My mom today is so beautiful, she looks ten years younger, maybe twenty. There is a difference between what walking in love and forgiveness will do in your life versus living in guilt. I didn't have to execute judgment—he was already serving his sentence. But when it was time, the judgment God wanted me to give—love—remains the same, "For vengeance is mine says the Lord."

Refusing to forgive and seeking revenge inhibits the anointing of God's Spirit in your life and the ability to change your circumstances. When I was a teenager, I tried to avenge my pain by being disrespectful and hurtful toward my parents. I did not accomplish what I wanted, which was for them to feel guilty and hurt for what they did to me. Proverbs 11:18 says, "He who sows wickedness reaps trouble." Acts of anger only beget anger. I thought acting out my pain would show my parents that they hurt me, and it would humble them and make them embrace me. But instead, it pushed them further away. No one wants someone being loud and disrespectful in their face whether they did something wrong or not. Acting out in anger only exasperates the situation. We can't bring good from operating out of the flesh. Only God can bring good out of bad, and He does it in the spirit.

On the other hand, love sown is love harvested. Galatians 6:7 says, "You reap what you sow." Proverbs 11:18 says, "He who sows righteousness is sure to reap a reward." Once I surrendered to God, He worked it out. I had to love and forgive to experience this love, peace, and joy. I had to love to be able to trust and stop walking in fear.

Ephesians 4:29-32 says,

> *Let no corrupt communication proceed out of your mouth, but that which is good to the use of edifying, that it may minister grace unto the hearers. And grieve not the Holy Spirit of God, whereby ye are sealed unto the day of redemption. Let all bitterness, and wrath, and anger, and clamor, and evil speaking, be put away from you, with all malice. And be ye kind one to another, tenderhearted, forgiving one another, even as God for Christ's sake hath forgiven you.*

Cry out to the Lord but allow Him to avenge your circumstances. Tell Him if you don't want to forgive and that you really want to see the person suffer (be honest with your pain and how you really feel). If you read Psalms, you will see that David did not hold back his tongue in asking God to avenge his enemies. The Bible is wonderful because it shows you that we all have trials, and we're all human. We all sin and get angry (Rom. 3:23). But if you read Psalms you will see when David cried out to God and confessed his anger, his heart was free again. After he was finished, he was speaking once again in faith, obedience, and praise toward God. He kept his eyes on and trust in God. He never avenged himself outside the will of God.

Romans 12:9-14 NKJV says,

Let love be without hypocrisy. Abhor what is evil. Cling to what is good. Be kindly affectionate to one another with brotherly love, in honor giving preference to one another; not lagging in diligence, fervent in spirit, serving the Lord; rejoicing in hope, patient in tribulation, continuing steadfastly in prayer; distributing to the needs of the saints, given to hospitality. Bless those who persecute you; bless and not curse.

This scripture is so powerful and key that I have to take a moment to discuss some parts of it.

The scripture above says "Cling to what is good." Think about plastic wrap and how tightly it clings to your bowl with no room for anything to get in or out. In the same way we are commanded to cling to what is good. There is no room for what you think or feel is good but only for what God says is good. We are to cling to what God says to develop the mind of Christ.

You must be fervent in the spirit, serving the Lord. To be fervent means to be eager, zealous, and passionate. The *Macarthur Study Bible* says, "fervent in the spirit literally means to boil over in the spirit." When it comes to serving God, you are supposed to be full of energy, readiness, and passion to please Him. Forgiveness is evidence that shows you are hot to please God, that love bubbles out of your mouth, and you are ready to obey Him.

Finally God's Word says rejoice, be patient in tribulations, be steadfast in prayer. To be steadfast means to be firm, un-wavering, and committed. You have to continually pray and ask God to help you. Prayer is your link to His power. Prayer is what gives your heart peace. We come in closest contact with God in His presence through prayer.

Ephesians 4:23-24 talks about renewing your heart and mind, and putting on the new man created according to God in righteousness and holiness. One missing key that prevents many from being transformed into a new (spiritual) man is that they can't emulate someone they do not know. It's hard to be holy and righteous when you don't understand what that means. Don't get me wrong, anyone who accepted Christ in their heart became righteous because of His righteousness. I'm talking about knowing how to walk in that righteousness. You have to make time for God through regular prayer, Bible reading, mediation, journaling, and praising Him.

Many Christians think holiness is just a behavior. But holiness is not external; rather it is internal. It is made possible through the desire of God to commune with us, from the blood of Jesus that covers us, and the indwelling of the Holy Spirit that reveals God to us and equips us to obey and be like Him. God is holy. Nothing we can do can make us holy. It is because God loves us so much He put some of his holiness in us so that He could be with us. The world and religion has deceived us to try to be holy through works. You are holy because God is holy. He chose us and made us holy too.

The reason I'm spending a little time with this is because in the same way you can't be holy or righteous if not for the spirit that indwells you, you can't forgive either without the spirit of God. Everything in you battles against the concept to forgive because it's unnatural to want to bless those that have hurt you.

This part of the journey is strictly spiritual. The world forgives, but it is in their own strength and so it's on their terms, and it doesn't bring the lasting healing they so desperately seek. The forgiveness that I'm talking about requires you to follow after God and walk in His power with a surrendered heart.

Part of forgiveness is to bless your enemies and don't curse them that persecute you. (I told you the ride would get bumpy at times.) It was hard to hear this because it made me accountable to God, and I had to take some responsibility in how long I stayed in my past. I'm writing to you as sister to sister and to brother, I know the pain and cross you carry is too heavy to carry in your human strength. Jesus says, "Come to me, all you who are weary and burdened, and I will give you rest. Take my yoke upon you and learn from me, for I am gentle and humble in heart, and you will find rest for your souls" (Matt. 11:28-29 NIV).

Does Not Gossip

Gossiping is when you use your past to make others look bad so that they will be ostracized and other people will stand with you. Will you choose to move forward or stay talking about the past? When you bring up your past, if it has no purpose but fleshly gratification, it's gossip. If it doesn't help you move into the light, it's gossip. If the conversation doesn't build the kingdom but divides and tears it apart, it's gossip. If the desired outcome is not to please God according to His will, it's gossip

I remember one day when I was about sixteen I was at my mother's job. During this time I was still carrying a lot of anger in my heart. My mother and I had a disagreement, and I had an angry outburst. I shouted out loud in front of her co-workers, "You're nothing; you let my stepfather molest

135

me." Now what healing could come out of telling that fact in such a terrible way? None. Also not only was this gossip but it was malicious, hurtful to everyone there and dishonoring to my mother.

You may be saying, "Well your stepfather did molest you." That's not the point. Not all gossip is false. It's how you use your conversation that makes it gossip. The point is there is a time, a place, and a way to handle your pain.

Now that I'm free, I'm trying to get you to see how to operate in the spirit and in love. This is about our responsibility and ability to not allow people, or our past, to hinder the blessings of our present. If you want to be blessed, you have to do it God's way. The solution is with Jesus. Your healing and accountability is between you and Jesus. Let's keep it simple. Don't focus on people in the past, hurl outbursts of anger at them, or try to change other people's opinion of them. The truth is that God doesn't bless those who have been hurt by giving them a pass to disregard the rest of His Word. He says honor your mother and father. It didn't say to do it if they never hurt you.

After I began to study God's Word, I realized that being hurt in my life did not give me the right to hurt others. I had no right to make anyone indebted to me. I had never died on a cross; I was only asked to trust God, obey Him, and carry my cross. God's Word says honor your mother and father. I'm sure I reaped some curses in my life because I was disrespectful to my mother. Just because we are hurt in life doesn't nullify God's Word. It doesn't give us the license to pick and choose what scriptures we will obey. In my pain God gave me grace, but I still suffered the consequences for disobedience.

Chooses To Be Merciful

The *New International Encyclopedia of Bible Words* says, "Mercy is love, reaching out to meet a need without considering the merit of the person that receives the aid." In other words, it is providing for someone's need, whether they are deserving of your help or not. In the Bible, mercy is expressed in not just feeling sorry for a person's affliction. No, a compassionate response should also follow (you would do whatever you could to help the person). There are many accounts in the Bible where people came to Jesus asking for mercy, and they were healed.

Receiving His help had nothing to do with the person asking for the help. Mercy was centered on the person able and willing to provide the help. God has been so merciful toward us. I know some of you may not yet feel this way because of what you have been through. For now, I'm asking you to believe that God has been merciful toward you, and He expects the same from us toward others. I was able to show mercy toward my stepfather and I did.

The greatest act of His mercy was stated in 1 John 4:10-11: "Herein is love, not that we loved God but that he loved us, and sent his Son to be the propitiation for our sins. Beloved if God so loved us, we ought to love one another." God loved us first; He made a way to redeem us and provide grace and mercy to us. Luke 6:36 tells us to be "merciful, as your Father also has been merciful." Furthermore, Matthew 5:7 says, "Blessed are the merciful for they will be shown mercy." Your blessings are directly related to how you bless others.

Chooses To Be Gracious

An act of graciousness is not always displayed by actions but can be expressed in the words we do not say. For instance, not condemning the person even though they are guilty is an act of graciousness as is not broadcasting to everybody what they did to us.

In the account of the adulterous woman caught in the very act of sin, she was guilty and brought by the men to be judged publicly. Look at how Jesus handled the situation. He simply kneeled on the ground, drew a circle in the dirt, and asked that the first person without sin throw a stone. Jesus could have condemned her; she was guilty and had sinned. He could have made her even more ashamed before the crowd, especially since He was the only one there without sin. However, He chose not to verbally condemn or humiliate her and therefore displayed an act of grace (John 8:10-11).

Before we go any further, I have said this is a spiritual walk now, and I'm assuming all of you know what I mean when I talk about the spirit of God. However, I'm being led to stop and say the same way some of you have walked in counterfeit forgiveness and didn't know it like me, some of you maybe are walking as counterfeit Christians. Wait, hear me out; I'm not judging you. But I don't want you to be deceived like I was and not do what's necessary to ensure you have really accepted Christ into your life. Many of you sincerely believe in Jesus. You like being around Him and gathering around His family. You like Him so much you may have even started serving in the church, maybe even got baptized.

Participation in ministry doesn't mean you have really accepted Jesus in your heart, and it doesn't mean you have made

Him Lord. There are a lot of you who think Jesus is good, you like His philosophies, but you don't really know Him. We call him by so many titles—baby Jesus, Lord, Messiah, Son of Man, Son of God—that you may not really know that He is God. Pray to God, and the Holy Spirit will reveal that truth to you. Even if you can't accept that right now, it's okay—it took me some time too.

One day when I was reading the scriptures, I clearly saw this truth and received it. But for now, just know that you need to really believe in Jesus, and it's more than an emotional or intellectual experience. Therefore, if He is Lord of your life, you will have the faith to follow in the things that He commands of us. Read Romans 10:9-11 and then meditate over this scripture. I want you to take some time and think about your relationship with Jesus. Acknowledge that you are a sinner. Today it's politically incorrect to say we are sinners, but if we're not, why would we even need a Savior? To save us from our own goodness?

The world wants you to believe that there are more ways to God than just through Jesus because then you wouldn't be accountable to Him. However, the Bible clearly says, "Jesus is the way, truth and life." I can't tell you how many people I have encountered who attend church but really do not know that Jesus is truly the only way. So God wanted me to extend an invitation for you to accept Him into your heart. You can do it right now where you are.

If you have not really accepted Christ in your life, you don't have the power of the Holy Spirit to finish this journey. Confess that you are a sinner, tell Jesus you need Him, you want Him to be Lord, and ask Him to show you the way. Ask Him to come into your heart, renew your mind (by thinking more like Christ), change and cleanse you, and forgive you so that you can forgive others. Then you will be officially a child of God. Think about this—the God Almighty, Creator of all life wants you! Join the family and never be alone.

A Matter of the Heart

Matthew 12:34 reminds us that whatever is in the heart will come out of the mouth. Proverbs 27:19 tells us that as a face is reflected in the water so does the heart reflect the person.

God showed me that forgiveness is a matter of the heart. I can't say this enough. The heart has been called the "seat of motivation." If you do not desire from the heart to act on something, you will not do it sincerely. Forgiveness has to be a real choice that you decide to make from the heart. I had to decide from my heart to forgive, wanting nothing in return, and holding no one accountable for my obedience to God but me. I had to want to see people blessed and not harmed from my actions because of my pain.

~ 10 ~

$\mathcal{O}$bstacles to Forgiveness

In every trip there are parts that are exciting, memorable, and enjoyable. Although the trip may be long, you were prepared and brought things to help you during those times when you were tired, restless, became aggravated, and sometimes wanted to turn back and go home when there still seemed to be more road ahead than was covered.

It's so funny that every time I have taken a trip, especially an automobile trip, it always seemed liked it took twice as long to get there than to return home. But the truth was the distance was the same, it's just easier to travel a road that you have been down at least once. So I'm telling you upfront, this part of the journey is the roughest, but stay focused. It will be easier the next time you have to travel it. Pain is inevitable, we encounter offenses daily. So remember the way.

Notice during the first part of the journey, the heart has to be prepared to forgive because pain stands in the way of obedience. In the second half, the focus is to show you how to forgive and stay single-minded in your decision to obey God. So if you need to take a break, a walk, exercise, or simply pray, just be determined to finish. There are many things about forgiveness I want to share; I wish I could share them all with you, but these are the issues that can easily become strongholds and prevent people from walking in forgiveness.

Helps the Offender Not To Be Overcome by Guilt

When I first shared this principle, there was a lot of resistance in the class. I even had some members leave and not return because I had forgotten about the journey in understanding this concept or wanting to obey it. This is why I will not present it self-righteously I promise; it wasn't easy just because God said it. No, it isn't; but nevertheless, we have to just trust God and obey. This principle was hard for me at first too. When God revealed to me that I had to help the person who hurt me not feel overcome by guilt, I thought, *Wait a minute, God. You are going too far with this forgiveness thing. You had me at first but now… Why should I have to care about the person to the extent that I want to help them not feel bad about what they did?* Thinking in the flesh, I couldn't see the larger picture. First of all, He said help them "not be overcome by guilt," which didn't mean they shouldn't feel remorse. They did need to feel a sorrow that leads to repentance just not condemnation. In His wisdom, He knew condemnation is ungodly guilt that gives the enemy access to deceive, torment, and keep us stuck.

The scripture says that I needed to help them not feel so overwhelmed by what they did that they felt tormented and couldn't move forward. When I was in the flesh, I thought, *Why not let them be tormented? They tormented me.* But now that I'm walking by the spirit, I see the wisdom that if you don't help them overcome their past, they remain who they are. What is the good in that? Sometimes people who hurt others feel too guilty to come to you to ask for forgiveness because they are too ashamed. How will you get that apology you have been waiting for, when the look in your eyes blasts out hate, anger, judgment, and condemnation? How can they approach you? Shame keeps people feeling unworthy to come to us or to God. The enemy then uses their shame as a stronghold in their life and keeps them from obtaining the saving faith and grace of God because they won't come to Him. The enemy keeps them separated from God and you.

These are not my words. Let's go to 2 Corinthians 2:6-7 where Paul talks about enough time had passed in which a person had been punished or disciplined in the church. "Now it was time to comfort, and contrariwise forgive so that the person doesn't become swallowed up from sorrow." I want you to look at the word "contrariwise." God is Himself acknowledging that to forgive and help a person who has done something wrong to us is contrary to our nature. We don't want to help someone who has hurt us. God is not insensitive, but we must trust and obey Him and His wisdom. He even provides the reason why we must help the person. Second Corinthians 2:10a, 11 reads: "To whom ye forgive any thing, I forgive also... Lest Satan should get an advantage of us: for we are not ignorant of his devices."

God is saying we have to forgive anything a person has done to us because He forgave all the things we have committed in our life through Christ. We forget that we are sinners ourselves, saved by the grace of God and in need of forgiveness from Him. Daily we sin, and God wants us to forgive as He has forgiven us.

Look at the next thing mentioned about why we should forgive. It says so that "Satan doesn't have an advantage over us." Paul said "to not be ignorant of devices that Satan uses against us." Unforgiveness is a device that the devil uses against us. We can't think that it's okay for God to forgive us and not show the same forgiveness and mercy toward others. It's a lie. The evidence of being a Christian is love and forgiveness. We can't keep being ignorant of the power of anger and unforgiveness in our life. It is a stronghold the enemy uses against us.

This account shows also that you can't indefinitely stay away from someone because they have sinned against you. The account says enough time had gone by so it was time to deal with the situation and the way was through forgiveness. If safety isn't the reason that prevents you from coming together, what is it? If you have been molested, you have to assess and test the person before you can be around them and certainly don't have your children around them. Please inform your children of people who can harm them. Or at least make every effort not to leave them unattended and alone. If the person is abusive, safety comes first. If someone has stolen from you, use wisdom and not trust them, but other than extreme circumstances, what is keeping you from forgiving and possibly reconciling (coming together and righting a relationship that went wrong)?

God commands us to forgive. We have to use wisdom and discernment to assess whether or not reconciliation can take place. Sometimes it can't or it may be delayed. You may have to assess whether or not the person can be trusted. Forgiveness and reconciliation are not the same. God doesn't want you or your children to be harmed. So I caution you where caution needs to be adhered to.

If you know someone who has been abused and they have

turned to a life of drugs, alcohol, or promiscuity stop looking at their behavior and judging them, find out their story and give them hope. We have to help one another and stop victimizing them all over again.

Conversations are going to have to get started. You're not the only one with pain. While you are going to be confessing, someone may come to you to confess the hurt that you did to them. Be humble, walk in God's grace and love, and let them get free. It's time to stop letting Satan use us against one another.

Doesn't Need an Apology

Needing an apology has been a large obstacle that has hindered people from wanting to forgive. Many people want an apology first before they can forgive. I did too. I have heard people say that they would forgive, but they wanted the person to seek their forgiveness first or admit what they had done. I wanted my mom to say she was sorry for not believing me. I wanted her to hold me and apologize. There's nothing necessarily wrong with wanting an apology, but when you allow it to stop you from obeying God or to keep you stuck, then it is a problem. When you really forgive, you don't need anything before you do it, not even an apology.

True forgiveness is an act of obedience and trust, whether the person ever admits that they are sorry. I was free before I saw my stepfather. I could have remained waiting for an apology and might have still been in bondage to unforgiveness.

Reconciliation and trust may not be able to take place until a person demonstrates that they have changed; but in order for forgiveness to take place, you need to say that you will no longer choose to be angry or seek revenge against them. You have cancelled their debt, and they do not owe you anything. Is an apology nice? Yes. Would it be wonderful if someone who hurt you acknowledges what they did to you first? Yes, but God didn't say an apology had to come first. If He did, His last words before He died on the cross would not have been, "Father forgive them."

God would have somewhere said that when a person apologizes then forgive. You won't find it in the Bible because it isn't there, although you will see accounts that show you how to use wisdom and discretion in walking in forgiveness and knowing when to reconcile and trust people who hurt you. (Read Genesis 37, 39-44, and 50.)

The following is an excellent, familiar account of a young man named Joseph who at the age of seventeen was beaten and sold into slavery by his brothers because they were jealous of their father's love for him and his dreams of a blessed future he shared with them. One bad thing after another happened to him. He was falsely accused and went to prison because a woman said he tried to rape her. He encountered these trials for more than fifteen years. But what helped him was that he knew God was with him.

After all that Joseph went through, God promoted him to be Prime Minister of Egypt. Due to a famine, his brothers eventually came to him for food, not knowing he was their brother. He wanted his family with him, but before he revealed himself to them and allowed them to stay, he had to test them. You see, I said before he could reconcile and allow them to come back safely into his heart, he had to test them.

When someone has hurt you they have to earn your trust but not your forgiveness; they have to earn the right to reconcile not receive forgiveness. Joseph had already forgiven his brothers before they even came for the food. If this wasn't so, he would not have been elevated to the second highest authority in Egypt. His heart was right with God and man. Some of you can't understand why you haven't been promoted to that next level. You have the education, experience, and skills. If you have all of that and haven't been promoted, maybe you need to ask God if your heart is right. Is there anyone you need to forgive?

What Happens When You Wait for an Apology?

I have a friend who was raped by her stepfather and became pregnant when she was seventeen. Her mother did not believe she was raped. She thought they had consensual sex, and as a result my friend and her baby girl had to leave home. As much as the rape hurt her, the fact that her mother did not believe her hurt her even more. Her parents stayed together. During most of her life, she was very bitter toward her mother. Yes, I know that my friend was abused and rejected. I could not even imagine going through what she did (someone's situation is always worse than your own).

Controlled by emotions, she eventually started using drugs and alcohol to numb her pain. She developed cirrhosis of the liver and hepatitis C. She lived with these diseases for many years before her health started failing. She stopped the drugs but she wouldn't let go of the drinking. She couldn't let the past go. She was a beautiful person until thoughts about her mother came up. She suffered one bad experience after another, living in anger and rebellion. Yes, she was hurt, but then she made choices that continued to cause her more pain.

She loved her child and she was a good mother. In fact that was the only child she had, and her daughter loved her so much. However, other than having her daughter, she was miserable. She stayed drunk to numb her pain. If she could have forgiven (given up) her past, she would not have had to drink her life away.

I remember talking to her over and over about forgiveness, telling her that she had to forgive her parents. She could not understand why she owed her parents anything, especially forgiveness. I told her that she had to deal with the pain, admit all the wrong, her feelings, and then, through God's grace, forgive what her parents did to her. She was so blinded by pain and anger that she didn't realize she was hurting herself.

She did not want to hear about trying to make their lives better. I had to help her see that forgiveness would make her life better. The enemy is subtle: if he can't destroy you, he will use devices (anger and unforgiveness) against us. No one had to hurt her further; she was doing it to herself and didn't know it. I talked with her about the negative choices she was making in her life. She said she would forgive if her mother would apologize. Oh I hated that stipulation because we can't make another person apologize to us. How long would she wait for someone to allow her to get free from her pain?

She did try to forgive but she wanted an apology, and when she wouldn't get it, she would become angry all over again. Years went by and her mother would not apologize. This tore my friend up even more than what happened in her past. You can't put yourself at the mercy of another person.

She was so focused on her pain that she didn't realize

time was not standing still for her. She was getting older with diseases that could potentially take her life. She needed to snap out of the past and be a mother to her daughter. I know you're thinking, *Yeah, but look at her life, she was hurt, betrayed.* I know, but staying angry was not going to change her past. However, forgiving would change her present, start decreasing the pain in her life, and allow her to take advantage of the time she had left. Actually, I didn't know what I know today about the journey through pain before you can cross into forgiveness, but it's okay because deliverance comes through Jesus.

Finally, after twenty years of suffering with the pain of her past, she decided to give it entirely to the Lord. She realized her mother was not going to admit what happened. My friend did not want to forgive during all those years because she thought it would excuse them of the wrong. However, God's Word says whatever a man sows he shall reap (Gal. 6:8). We are not God and we have to stop trying to be God.

Unable to fight in her own strength any longer, my friend gave her pain over to God (1 Pet. 5:7) and allowed Him to help her. She forgave her mother wholeheartedly. You might be thinking, *Why does the person that was wronged have to carry the responsibility for this total act of forgiveness?* Why? Because the person living with an unforgiving heart is the one who continues to suffer and be tormented from the past. Living with pain and anger caused her to make choices that brought her harm in her present. If you want to be blessed, there is no other way but to forgive (Matthew 5:7) and not allow an apology to hold you captive to your past.

When my friend forgave in God's way, she began to experience blessings in her life. She had peace, joy, and love again.

After she stopped harboring resentment, she was free to laugh again. (Stay with me, I know this is hard to digest, but it's the truth.) God's Word is truth. I am a testimony, and so was my friend. She did die from complications of cirrhosis in 2014, but she had happiness and peace before her death. She had reconciled with her family after she stopped waiting for an apology. The love she wanted, her family didn't know about, otherwise she would not have been in the situation she was at seventeen. But thanks be to God, she finally submitted so He could show her what real love is, and she received it. When she received it, she helped her family not be overcome with guilt and her mother got saved before she died, and they both were attending church together.

Because she forgave her mother God's way (freely), eventually her mother did admit what happened before she died. When my friend had forgiven her mother, she did not want her mother to suffer in guilt like she had in anger. The devil wasn't going to use devices of anger and shame in their lives anymore. The door that had them both in darkness was closed. Love is pervasive; bringing freedom to each person it touches. My heart is filled with tears as I think about the transformation in my friend's life and how the dynamics changed between her and her mother. That is the power of God's love.

Gets Rid of Bitterness

Bitterness is an inward condition. R.T. Kendall says it develops when there is "an excessive desire for vengeance that comes from deep resentment." S. Arterburn said regarding forgiveness that "It is at the core of our emotional being." Further, he says that "Emotional pain never dies a natural death and we can't kill it by burying it. If we try to bury it while it is still alive, it will kick and scream until we acknowledge it, feel it, and put it behind us through forgiveness. Unforgiving people are emotionally sick. Their bitterness is a disease of the spirit, and it is inevitable that the unforgiving person will eventually experience physical illness as well."

The ability to forgive is not passive; it requires action. God already knows how we handle situations when we are hurt. He knows that we internalize the pain and allow bitterness to take root in our hearts. If that wasn't the case, He would not have told us to "put away all bitterness" (Eph. 4:31-32). As soon as we get angry, we have to confess it, deal with it, and give it to God before it takes root. Don't let your anger become fertile in your heart.

You have to stop the roots from growing and extract those vines out of your life. John 15:1-3 tells us that Jesus is the vine, any branch connected to Him will produce good fruit, and you will be made clean through His Word. We can purge the weeds in our lives from the bitter roots that have grown in us by abiding in Christ and his love. We must allow God's love to take root in our hearts.

Unforgiveness Is Idolatry

This was one I didn't want to discuss, but I have to tell you the truth of everything God is leading me to say. I know normally when we hear the word "idolatry," it isn't associated with unforgiveness. However, God says that He is a jealous God and not to have any other gods before Him—craven images or otherwise. I heard a prominent person say she was offended by that statement. For God to say that He was jealous, in her mind, it reduced Him to the level of a human instead of elevating Him to be recognized and honored above all other gods. When we have thoughts, beliefs, imaginations, agreements, or arguments that exalt themselves in our life over what God is telling us, then we have engaged in idolatry (2 Cor. 10:3-5).

When God says to forgive and a thought in your mind tells you not to forgive for whatever reason, that thought becomes idolatrous because it is trying to cause you to step outside of God's Word and will and is trying to make itself superior to God.

You will decide what god you will serve by positioning yourself on the battlefield in your mind. Yes, the enemy speaks to us in our minds. If you have a thought that is contrary to the will and word of God, you are supposed to cast it out and bring it into obedience to Christ. You do that by speaking the truth and light (God's Word). His Word says we have to forgive; it is not optional. If we humble ourselves despite our feelings and pain, we show that we serve God almighty.

However, if you accept the thought that tells you not to forgive, you have chosen to believe another god's words. Whether you realize it or not, you are on the enemy's side. The Bible says you can't serve two masters (Matt. 6:24).

Idolatry basically is an expression of human pride, an independence from God, a way of thinking that allows man to trust and direct his own life. I did not like this truth when God first put it in my spirit. However, if I wanted to heal, I had to accept all of God's truth. There was no more pity partying days with God. When He healed me, He prepared me for duty, and I'm accountable to give you His Word to set you free too—all of it, the parts you want to hear about His love and the parts you may not want to hear about—forgiveness.

Forgiving God

Some of you may not even realize that you are angry with God. I know you do not want to admit this and for some reason not too many people will allow you to be that honest, but you must. Some of you are mad at God, and you're not afraid to admit it, and it's hard to come to Him for help. It's okay, God is your Father; He knows you. If you can't speak it, then write it. Just get it out. Remember, 1 John 1:9 says to confess your sin before God, and He is faithful to cleanse you and make you righteous. Having unforgiveness in your heart toward God is a sin.

You can't fellowship with God in sin. The Bible says we can be angry but sin not. Anger become sin when 1) it causes you to question the sovereignty of God; 2) it leads you to rebel against His word; 3) it causes you to run away from Him; 4) you dethrone Him as God; 5) you serve another god; 6) you become your own god; 7) you no longer see Him as God.

Despite your pain, He wants you to trust Him, stay in His love, and obey Him. You can question Him but don't allow your reasoning to doubt Him or lead to unbelief. In order for you to get help, you have to go before God. If you have animosity in your heart toward God, confess it because your prayers will not be heard or answered otherwise. He knows your heart. Maybe this is the reason why your relationship with God seems stale, dry, or distant. In the same way when standing at the altar, if there is any unforgiveness in your heart toward someone and you have gifts, you must first lay your gifts down. Before God will hear from you, you have to try to resolve anger in your relationships. If there is any separation in your heart against God you must take the same step. Start first by confessing any wrong thinking in your heart against God and get it right. It's the same principle. Confess your anger toward Him so that He will bless you.

God doesn't need our forgiveness. In fact we can't really forgive God because He is perfect and without sin. But I say that I had to forgive Him in my humanness, because that is what we need to do as humans in order to move on. I felt hurt by God, not that He caused my hurt but He didn't stop it. Nevertheless, until I confessed it, my heart was still blocked. So God said if you have anything against anyone, confess it. Anyone is anyone, including Him. He knows that fellowship with Him can't continue until we confess our pain and anger and allow Him to clean our heart again whether that is to a person or toward Him. Unforgiveness carries the same burden and penalty—no fellowship with Him. So in His grace whatever is on our heart, whoever we hold anything against (man or God), He tells us to make it right. I believe that included Him.

The one thing I have to interject is that God didn't cause your pain. Although for reasons we may never know or understand, He did allow it. He is perfect and without sin. He is not subject to us. Let me not get it twisted. He was working things out for the good and His glory. It took thirty-five years for me to fully see and understand why I had to take this journey. By forgiving God I was able to stand in His presence and see Him again. If you forgive God, you too will be able to see Him despite the death of a loved one, loss of a marriage, tragedy, illness or whatever pain you may be experiencing in your life. Forgive and let God be God so He can use His power, love and wisdom to help you get through.

Oh God just summed it up for me. Giving me permission to feel like I could forgive Him took away my power or desire to make Him indebted to me. To forgive means I had to cancel His debts (although He never had any). I couldn't keep trying to make Him subject to me or owing me. Canceling His debts means we can't think in our minds or heart that He owes us anything. If He doesn't owe us anything, there should be no more questions and reasonings before we obey Him. It doesn't mean you can't bring Him your heart, it just means you can't make Him subject to the emotions of your heart any longer. We simply allow Him to be God in our lives and trust in His love. God canceled our debts too. In forgiveness no one owes anything but love.

~ 11 ~

*F*orgiveness:
The End of My Story

As you can tell, I am a storyteller. I want to share with you what love looks like in my family today by sharing the kind of relationship I now have with my mom and dad. I have been excitedly waiting to share this part with you. I can say unequivocally that forgiveness and love work. What I always wanted from my parents, I have experienced and then some because I learned to love like Jesus and stopped putting stipulations on them.

I gave the reins to God, respected my parents regardless of the past, and today I am so in love with my parents and they are with me. When I was in pain I couldn't see who they were—I only saw how they disappointed me. I had forgotten who my mother was, and I didn't know my father. But the last twenty years have been good, and the last ten great. As I've gotten to know both of my parents, I've learned about some of their scars from their past that shaped them too. We all have a story. I'm just glad that we didn't allow our pain to keep us stuck.

God says that He uses all things to work out for the good

for His purpose for those who love Him (Rom. 8:28). I didn't believe that years ago, but I have seen God's faithfulness. He used all my pain and my past to help complete me. How? I know how to stand in the midst of trials instead of falling apart and cursing God. I know how to use the trials in my life, remain steadfast in His love, and use it for His glory.

Let me share one last story with you that brought my whole life full circle. One day I was feeling short of breath at work and having a little chest pain. So I left early and went to the emergency room and my husband, Magic, met me there. The doctor ordered a CT Scan of my lungs. Instead of giving me a CT Scan of my chest, the technician mistakenly performed a CT Scan on my head. I didn't realize they were scanning my brain because I just wasn't paying any attention. When I came back to my holding room, the ER doctor looked at my films. He was upset and asked, "Who ordered me a CT Scan of her brain?" On the order, instead of indicating CT Scan for the chest, written on it was, "CT Scan for the head to rule out aneurysm of the brain." The amazing thing is no one wrote that order, not the ER physician or the radiologist! Another God moment—He is always present in our storms.

While the doctors and nurses were arguing over the mistake and trying to figure out who was going to pay for the unordered test, I was just thinking, *I want to get out of this place and go to another hospital. They're just trying to get money out of me. I'm not paying for any extra test.* The physician returned to me saying that they didn't know who ordered that test or why, but since it was done, I was going to have to pay for it and they would try to work out something with me. Oh I wasn't having that at all; I was not paying for anything. I forgot my chest was hurting; I just wanted to get out of that crazy hospital. But one of the nurses, God love our nurses, she told me to look at the bottom of the report. I did and there was an important finding discovered, and she suggested that I should follow it up with my primary doctor.

I wasn't going to do it at first, but something in my spirit said, "Go check it out." See how love works—God was there with me, guiding and protecting me, and leading me to go to the doctor. So I followed up with a neurologist and he ordered an MRI. After I had it, he said he would follow up with me in a few days with the results.

I never suspected that there would be a problem. The day when I was to hear the results, I was doing my daily Bible study. I was reading the Numbers 11, which was talking about the Israelites complaining to Moses because they wanted to eat something different. They were tired of eating only the provision (manna), the miraculous bread from heaven that God had supplied for His hungry people in the dry, barren land.

God told Moses that He was going to give them enough meat for a month. Moses questioned how God could feed over 600,000 men, not including women and children, for such a length of time. Moses said, "If we slaughtered all of our animals and herds or fished for all the fish in the sea, there would still not be enough." That's why we can't rationalize against God's Word with our wisdom. However, what God said to Moses really blessed me in that moment.

The Lord said, "Is the Lord's arm too short? You will now see whether or not what I say will come true for you" (verse 23). I was just meditating over those words "Is my arm too short?" In other words, God was reminding Moses that there are no limitations with Him and nothing was impossible. It took me to another part of the Bible that says of God, "He is able to accomplish more than we would ever dare to ask or hope" (Eph. 3:20 NLT). I was feeling so secure and thankful to know that I had the all-powerful God Jehovah in my life. Just as I was saturating my mind with this truth, the phone rang. It was the neurologist.

He asked, "Are you alone?" I said "Yes." He said, "Sit down, your test came back abnormal for a brain aneurysm." I was shocked. I didn't know what to say or do, so I just let the doctor keep on talking. He asked if I was still there because I was so quiet. When I got off the phone, I wanted to fall apart. But something inside of me wouldn't let me do that. I couldn't think, "Why me, God?" or, "You must not love me, God." I had experienced the truth and light in my life. I knew that God had redeemed me from my past, and I was not going back there. The only thing I could do was turn to God, stay in Him, and walk in the faith that He had taught and placed in me. I stayed in His love; I didn't look to the left or the right. I would not allow circumstances to stumble me again.

You might be thinking, *What does this have to do with forgiveness?* Wait. I will get to the wonderful love my parents provided for me. I would need surgery, a craniotomy to put a clip on the aneurysm and prevent it from rupturing, which would be life threatening. I was so scared. I couldn't imagine having anyone cut open my head. I decided I wasn't going to do it. I was just going to let the doctors follow up through CT Scans and watch it. My in-laws flew in from California to convince me that I had to have the surgery. My mother-in-law said I was playing Russian Roulette; if and when it burst, that could be my life. My mother just kept praying and telling me to have faith.

For days, maybe weeks, I kept debating whether or not I would have the surgery or not. Fear was gripping me. One night while I was asleep, I went to bed with surgery on my mind. I was restless, tossing and turning. And in my spirit it was so clear; it was like God was face to face with me. He said, "I revealed it to you while it was small. Do you want it to grow? Do you want it to burst? You didn't have a choice over your past. I'm letting you have a choice. It's not an emergency. You can walk in there and have your surgery." Then He asked again, "Do you want it to grow?" I said no!

The next morning I woke up confident that God was going to be with me, although I was still afraid. I told my family that I would have the surgery and it was scheduled. I just couldn't imagine having my head cut open. For some reason the neurologist had to cut from the top mid-front of my skull, down the whole right side of my head, across my right ear, and across the right length of the right side of my neck.

Let me show you how forgiveness allowed my parents to bless me. Had I not gone through this situation, I never would have understood the love and power of God in my life, or how much my parents really loved me. I started my story by sharing the pain and brokenness in my relationships. I felt that my parents never sacrificed for me or made me feel secure or protected, so I'm glad I get a chance to share a different end to the story.

The day of my surgery I had so many family and friends with me that we needed three waiting areas! It was a blessing to me in and of itself that so many people would be there for me. As a little girl who always felt alone, it was beautiful having such a full life surrounded by so many people. I realized when you are walking in love, there is a radiance that draws people to you. When you give love, it will come back to you. Forgiveness is a vehicle to bring love to you.

While everyone was in the family lounge, my mother didn't talk or socialize with anyone—she stayed in the chapel praying for me. My mother is and always has been a praying woman, who has strong faith. I know it saved me from taking my life with my ex, and I knew God would listen to her prayers now. I judged her faith when I was growing up because of some of the choices she made, but I have learned that we can't judge the heart through a person's actions necessarily. My mother was the one who taught me to believe in God and to make Him real. I first heard my mother supplicating on the behalf of her children when we needed food, were going wayward, or were hurting. My mother introduced God to me as a Father, and I will always be thankful to her for that.

My mother doesn't play when it comes to praying for her children. She doesn't want any distraction. It is just her and God. When it comes to pleading for her children and going before God because she knows her child is in serious trouble and only He can help, she will be relentless until she feels peace and has assurance that her child will be okay.

She had come up for a few days earlier before my surgery. While visitors were coming to the house, my mom stayed in seclusion, warring in prayer for me. She couldn't lose focus by the distractions of other people. She didn't do this out of guilt—it was out of love.

She stayed away in the chapel praying to God for me

until I came out of surgery. I just want you to see the love that this woman, my mother, has for me, the love that I would have never known or have been able to experience had I not forgiven. After I came out successfully, and all my visitors left, my mother begged the nurse if she could just sit in a chair inside my room a little longer. I was okay, the surgery had gone well, but my mother just wasn't ready to leave her baby. My mother stayed those first few nights, barely eating and not leaving my side. She was covering me with her prayers and love.

I had the loving support of many others, including my wonderful husband, daughters, friends, in-laws, church family, my sister Summer, and co-workers, but I'm only sharing about my parents at this point. My mother would not leave my side. This was so important to me because I had forgotten that my mother could be tender, loving, and make me feel special. But that is who my mom is—she makes everybody feel special and important. I can remember how she fed the homeless and took in orphans and family members who needed help. I hated that I had allowed a moment in time to erase all my other memories of this beautiful woman. From this point ten years ago, I want to say she has been my BFF (best friend forever), but my girls will get jealous and say I'm their BFF (you can't have too much love). In unforgiveness you only remember what hurt you. For so many years I believed my mother didn't love me and wouldn't protect me. But she did valiantly protect me that night when she threw my stepfather out of the house.

For so long I had only remembered the day when I didn't feel her protection, and I forgot that it wasn't always like that. I had a heart of bitterness, blame, and anger. I condemned and pushed my mother away most of my teen years, and this prevented my mother and me from expressing love toward each other. Now through forgiveness and a situation that only God could bring good out of, we were together more intimately than we had ever been. I had never seen my mother cry like this for me and pray to the point of weakness. She wasn't praying in fear—she was fighting for me in her authority, in love, to let the enemy know he could not have me.

After my surgery I stayed in the hospital for only four days and was discharged home. The only major problem I had was that, during the surgery, the nerve behind my right eye was nicked and I developed palsy. I had double, blurred vision and could not see well for several months. Other than being weak and needing assistance around the house, I was recovering well. However, about two weeks later, I developed some complications and had to be rushed back to the hospital. I had developed fluid in both of my lungs, a blood clot in my left leg, several blood clots in my right lung, had liver toxicity, and I was in excruciating pain.

My mother was back in Detroit because I was recovering so remarkably at first that I had told her to go home. Suddenly I received overwhelmingly bad reports from the doctors. Fear was starting to encompass me. I called my mother and told her all that was going on with me. I said, "Mom, I'm going to die. There is no way I can make it out of this." My mother's response shocked and angered me, but it was the jolt I needed to remember from Numbers 11 that "God has no limits."

She asked who was I to be God and decide His plan for my life, and who said I was going to die. Then to top it off she asked me, "Where is your faith?" I thought she was being so insensitive. I had forgiven her from the past so I didn't go back there, bringing up old records. But I did feel hurt. I was thinking, *What is wrong with her? I just had major surgery and now I have major complications. These are real issues. What does this have to do with faith? I was dying.* Now, I know everything in life, every feeling, reaction, and action is centered off our faith. But I didn't know it at the time. That's why I said I had to experience some things before I completed this book.

When I got off the phone with my mother, I soaked for a moment in pity. But then the Holy Spirit asked, "Where is your faith? Didn't I reveal the aneurysm to you? I wrote the order for the doctor to do the CT Scan. I carried you through the surgery." And He reminded me of so many trials He had walked me through in the past. So as I laid there, a peace came over me. I felt secure in Him and told Him I would trust Him. It was about my faith. I needed to keep walking in it and not stop just because of my circumstances. I needed my mother to remind me to remember my faith, not that I didn't have faith.

I started thinking about all that God had done for me. I told my husband to bring my Bible and gospel music in so I could listen to it. My vision was still blurry in my right eye so everyone read the Bible to me. My faith started to energize me. I needed my mother. I had been speaking death over myself. If the enemy couldn't do it alone, he just needed for me to agree with him and give up the will to live, like he had tried before. My mother spoke life into me!

My dad was so cute during all of this too. He is so proper and likes to be called doctor, but now he wasn't caring about anything but me. My father never was a very religious person. I didn't know if he believed in God. I knew he attended church once in a while with his wife (my stepmother whom I love). I had never seen my father pray or really talk about God other than when I brought Him up.

My dad liked always being in control but now found himself praying more to God. My father said he prayed more to God during this time than in his whole life. He came to the hospital every day to see me and stayed until visiting hours ended. In the past if he hadn't put it on his schedule, he wasn't going to do it. And now he was coming every day, allowing my welfare to interrupt his plans, and I didn't even have to ask.

My father read my Bible to me, and would read it as long as I wanted because that was my life. He knew I needed to hear from God. He knew the only way I was going to make it was to have God next to me, and he didn't hesitate to invite my big Daddy in. I knew while he was trying to comfort me with the Bible that it was comforting him too.

My mom wanted to come back to be with me, but every time she tried, she got sick. God wouldn't allow her to come back for a while. He just allowed her and I enough time to experience love, but He didn't want her to get all of His glory, and He knew I had to spend time with my father. I had to get to know his heart, the man underneath all of that façade of being cool and not showing a lot of emotions. He has a heart of gold, and he is very sensitive. I just had to get to know him and not critique how I thought he should be.

When I was released this time from the hospital, I had different people stay with me for scheduled periods of times. I had my Auntie Denise, my in-laws, and my mother was released to come back, and my father came and stayed with me. I have four bedrooms and he could have slept in his own room, but my daddy slept in a chair next to my bed when it was his turn. He didn't want to leave me alone. He fixed me food, helped set it up for me, went to the grocery store, helped the girls with homework, and of course read my Bible to me.

I saw the concern in my father's eyes when I looked at him. For the first time I saw that I really mattered to him; he didn't want to lose me. I saw that he would have experienced a void in his life if I wasn't in it. He had become Grandpa for the first time to two beautiful girls (we didn't have the other children during this time, just the girls). Even in his fear for me, he had such a strength and calmness about him. I felt safe with him. I love you, Daddy. I'm so glad you were there with me.

The pressure and pain were so great in my head that I could not go up the stairs, bend down, sit on the toilet, or even bathe myself. My mother left everything and came to help. She had her own business, taught at a high school, and had returned to college, but she was determined to stay with me for as long as it took. Some of you may be thinking, *What is so special about that?* Remember, I said previously, I resented my mom because I felt that she loved her husband more than me, that she put him before our family.

Therefore, I never thought that she would sacrifice anything for me. That's what anger will do—it will cause you to compartmentalize everything based on one experience. I felt that since my mother didn't believe me, which hurt me in the past, she would always fail me. That was my past thinking. I have had many wonderful times prior to my surgery with my mom and dad, but I am using this story to show you how different we are today.

I never would have thought to ask my mother to sacrifice

her dreams for me. My mom had not graduated high school, she had six children and had to work hard all of her life. Now she was living her dream. She had received her G.E.D. and gone to college to get her bachelor's in education and opened several businesses. Even though we had a good relationship now, I did not know if she would put her dreams on hold. I wanted her to be there with me, but I could not imagine her putting her future on hold again. I was happy and proud of her for pursuing her education. Now that I was healthy spiritually, I didn't want her to miss out on her dreams after all she had been through. When you're not thinking about your pain, you're not operating in selfishness. I wasn't just thinking about me anymore.

As soon as she could work it out, she was back here with more suitcases and clothes than my entire household. She was in college but she said nothing was going to stop her from taking care of me. She made me feel certain that there was absolutely nothing more important than me. This is an example of the fruits of forgiveness: both parties think about the other person; both parties want what's best for the other and have genuine peace about it. I've learned that we all love differently, and our perception of love is shaped from all of our total experiences. But there is a love that is immeasurable—the love of Christ.

Genuine forgiveness releases the person completely from any debts. She didn't owe me anything, and because I loved her now through Christ, I did not have selfish love. I did not want her to miss out on her dreams, but she said that I was a part of her dreams; we were a part of each other.

My mother would read the Bible and spiritual books every day to me because she knew how important God's

Word was for me. I would wake up at night and my mother would not have even gone to bed; when it was her turn, she was in the rocking chair all night in my room, praying and watching over me. She and my father wouldn't take the guest bed—when it was their turn, they stayed up all night watching over me.

When I think back, it's surreal sometimes how much my mom and I were connected. I remember singing a song in my subconscious while asleep and when I'd awaken, we'd both be humming the same spiritual song. I experienced what I had always wanted from my mother: protection, being put first, love, connection, and time. Through forgiveness, I was able to experience that and so much more. Now I want to share a little more about my father during this time.

After my mother returned home, my father came to my home every day from work. This is extraordinary for my father because he follows schedules so rigidly. My father prides himself on his work ethics. He always brags about the fact that he does not call off work, in fact he had accumulated enough sick days to get paid for three full years. However, that all changed with my illness. He rotated with my husband in taking me to my follow-up doctor visits, and he would have taken off work if I needed him to do so. This was a true act of love on my father's part for me. I've learned to accept people's love how they can give it.

Once I saw an e-poem titled "An Interview with God," and one of the things it said was that God wanted us to know that there are a lot of people waiting to love us, but they just do not know how to do it. This was true for my father—he did not know how to love me when I was a child. If I had closed my heart with an unforgiving spirit, then I would have not been able to receive it later when I so needed it. Later is better than never. I love my father, and I hope that if any of you have estranged relationships with your father, you'll allow him to come back. Hear their story too. It doesn't make it right what they did in the past, but it helps you to understand them better. There are a lot of parents who have regrets for the past. Let's stop punishing them and hurting ourselves.

My father read my Christian books to me (God was still working things out in our lives). Everything that we go through is not always just about us. Sometimes God is using your life or circumstances to reach His other children (we may be the vessel to get them to see God). As much as I was angry at my father in the past, I would not want him to have gone to hell. That is where God wants our heart—to love a person enough that despite what has happened in our life, we care where they will spend eternity. God wants all of us to receive everlasting life through belief in Christ and love others with renewed minds and hearts.

God used my illness to not only give me my father for the first time all to myself, but ultimately God used this time now that I wasn't twisted or broken or in darkness for me to share the gospel with my father. I love my father. I want him to receive salvation. What better testimony of the gospel than to still praise God in the midst of a storm. He saw my faith at work.

For the first time, my father was connecting with me and God. I really experienced the love of my father. He put nothing before me. It happened through forgiveness. Forgiveness releases you to release others and let God work it all out. I'm so glad that God gave me my family. I always prayed for a family and now I have just that—the love of my parents, a real Christian husband who loved me through my mess, my children and most importantly, God who never left me, even when I left Him.

The same way I did not think I would survive my childhood, I did not think at times I would survive this ordeal, but God showed me truly that He does not put more on us than we can handle. I am a living testimony. Like I said before, had I not experienced this situation I would have never been able to portray the loving, giving, sacrificing, and faithful parents that I have today. What changed us all from the past? The power of forgiveness enables you to love unconditionally through God, for God, and because of God.

I have a poem that my father wrote to me a couple years ago. This truly is an expression of what forgiveness looks like. Although the word forgiveness is never mentioned, subtly he asks for it, and the love he says I gave him shows that he received it. But he gave it to me also.

My Daughter, I Am Grateful to You

For staying, although I had turned
Away, I am grateful to you
For having the unconditional Love that you convey,
I am grateful to you
For being willing to listen
Though I held you at bay
I am grateful to you
For keeping track of me
When I had gone astray
I am grateful to you
For understanding that in
Life we must learn and reflect

From day-to-day, I am
Grateful to you
For having wisdom to know
That amongst the black and
White situations of life
There remains preponderance
Of gray, I am grateful to you
For having the belief in us
Which is a position from,
Which you would not sway,
I am grateful to you
My daughter, you are a precious
Gift to me, a needed irreplaceable
Part of my life, I am eternally
Grateful to you for helping
Me find my way
        —*Your Father*

I think that this poem perfectly says what forgiveness does. The person who forgives is free to love even when they do not receive it back. They can help others not be overcome by guilt so that ultimately they too can repent, come to God, love, and receive it (2 Cor. 2:7). Love freed my father to not be imprisoned by guilt for leaving me. He was able to have the confidence to offer his heart and not fear rejection from me. My father says that through me he learned how to love because I would not give up on him. Actually my father is giving me too much credit. It wasn't that I was able to love so strongly, powerfully, or righteously. I had learned how to love through God, and my father felt God's love through me. He experienced the overflow of God's Holy Spirit—that's what released him from feeling guilty and taught him how to love.

My love was selfish. I wanted him to love me—how I wanted to be loved and have him pay me back for hurting me. That's why I would argue and disrespect him when he would come to visit when I was a teenager. But when I allowed God to get in me, my heart changed. I stopped praying for what I wanted people to give me because God showed me that I had to give something first. I protested for a while. *Why me first?* But He showed me that I couldn't understand some things, I just needed to trust and obey.

When you open your heart, you will receive that which you desire—LOVE. God's fruit began to grow in my life, and instead of receiving my rotten fruit (anger, fear, revenge, and bitterness), everyone was reaping love, forgiveness, kindness, compassion, joy, and peace—the fruit of God's Spirit (Gal. 5:22-23). I am not perfect, but now that I know how to forgive, I try to walk daily in it. The old person tries to resurface her ugly head, but I fight the temptation with the Spirit and the Word of God and resist going back to the past and being bitter again (Eph. 4:31-32).

There was an account in the Bible when Moses went on the mountain and spoke with God and his whole countenance changed. In fact, his hair turned white and his face had a powerful glow. When he came off the mountain, people knew he had been in the presence of the Lord—they could see it; in fact, he had to cover his face because some of God's glory was still upon him. Too often, we say that we know the Lord or that we've been with the Lord: we go to church, pray, study the Bible, but no one can tell we have been in the presence of the Lord. We may not have a glow like Moses after being in God's presence, but there should be some evidence.

What evidence is there today that you've been in the presence of God? Forgiveness is a true sign of whether or not we belong to God or have been in His presence. Forgiveness is that glow that shines upon your face when you have been in the presence of God. You cannot be in the presence of Love (God does not have love—He is Love) and not come out loving; it is impossible!

My parents not only took care of me during my time of illness, but they are very involved in my life today. They are excellent grandparents. Through forgiveness, I did not continue to foster generational curses on my children by keeping them estranged from people they need to know and love. I'm not teaching my children to hate and fear, but to trust and love through God. It was my youngest daughter when she was a young girl who made me call my father Dad. Up until that point I was calling him by his name. She said "No, Mommy, that doesn't sound right; that isn't respect." I was waiting for the feeling in my heart and she said, "No, follow what you have taught us from God's Word." It's funny—obedience changed my heart.

Everybody loves my mother; she is so charismatic, beautiful, caring, and loving, and all the kids run to her. I'm glad my children are a part of that. My mother is like a magnet. Everyone in her presence feels special, beautiful, and empowered. She is the most positive and faithful person that I know. I'm glad that I did not allow my past to blind and imprison my mind from who she is today. My mother did not always make the best decisions, but I do not have to bring that up anymore; it is truly in the past—the book is finished.

My father is so smart. He is like a walking library. Anytime my children or I need help with information, we all know to call Grandpa. My father never used to be an affectionate person; he never showed emotion through hugs and kisses. Neither could you tell what he was feeling; he would always keep a blank face, even when I would cry my heart out to him as a child. I resented that about him. Today, my father cannot stop kissing me and my children. I can see when he is sad, afraid, happy, or sorry; he shares his heart with me now. Wow! Like God said, His Word sets free those that are captive (Luke 4:18). The past no longer holds us anymore. My father even has a sense of humor and we have pet names for each other. He allows me to love him fully, and in turn, he is able to do the same. There is no pain blocking our hearts.

There is no fear in my heart anymore with my father. I am able to be me. I do not fear anymore if I say something he doesn't like that he will cast me out of his life. I am a part of his life, heart, and legacy. We both realize without each of us, we could not experience the fullness of whom we were to become. God has set us all together in this journey. I love my father and he loves me. He doesn't expect me to be perfect. He knows I love God more than anything, but I will make mistakes and he has learned to cover me with grace in those times.

Well, this is the end of my story, and I want to share a revelation I just received from my mother. This is another confirmation for why we need to take this journey. It came just before the final edit, thirty-five years from when I first started this journey. I was sharing some things about the book with my mom, and we were crying and laughing. She wasn't aware of the pain I had experienced with my first husband and my religion, and she asked me why I hadn't told her. I confessed that it was because as a child when I told her my pain about my stepfather, she didn't believe me so I never shared my heart with her again. I couldn't believe what she said next. She told me that she did believe me, but at the time she too was studying with that same religious organization and had gone to the Elders for counsel and they told her not to leave her husband but to keep her family together and make it work. Wow...I wished I had known this back then. She believed me! That same religion that I later attached myself with had influenced her too. Boy, the pain and rejection and anger I had felt all of those years, thinking she didn't believe me. God could have allowed me to know this back then, but then I wouldn't be able to tell you that you could be free without apologies. You could be free just from confessing your pain to Him, surrendering your anger, and walking in love. I had to take the journey to share with you the truth about forgiveness. Thanks, Mom, for sharing this with me. I love you so much.

You see everything isn't what you think, no matter how dark it looks. Take the journey and discover the answers to unlock your heart and set you back on the path that pain tried to divert you from. Destiny still calls... Today my mother and I travel to different places sharing our message "One Love, One Community," bringing love back into families.

Forgive, Bless, and Be Blessed

Do you want to be blessed? Do you want to have restoration in your life and relationships like I have had with my family? It's never too late. I wish I had some special revelatory catchy phrase to end with but I don't. The following may sound like a religious cliché, but it is the truth so I must say it. If we want to be blessed, it all boils down to not allowing our pain to distort our hearts or perceptions about God, ourselves, and the world around us. I know life isn't fair and it hurts sometimes. I'm not going to tell you that you will never experience pain again. But I can promise you that if you confess your pain, don't allow anger to hold you captive and unforgiveness to become a stronghold in your heart but rather trust God, stay in His love, obey His Word, and choose to forgive wrongs, you will be blessed.

The Bible says that after Job confessed his pain, repented, and worshiped God, he was asked to do something. God told Job that because He was angry at his friends for what they said, He wanted Job to offer up sacrifices and go pray for them. In other words, God wanted Job to bless (forgive) them. God knew what was in his heart. He was offended and felt betrayed by his friends. They hurt Job too.

Job had a decision to make. Despite his pain, he had experienced the true presence of God. If God was his Lord and if now he really knew God like he said, there would be only one response in his decision. After Job obeyed and prayed for them, the Bible says his blessings came, "The Lord restored his fortune." There is no getting around it. If you want to be blessed, you are going to have to obey God and forgive those who have hurt you. But there is no comparison to what you will receive in return.

The Lord gave Job twice as much as he had before! "Then all his brothers, sisters, and former friends came and feasted with him in his home..." (see Job 42:1-12). The scripture goes on to say how the second part of Job's life was even better than the first. Today I have seen this worked out in my own life because I now have a relationship with all my siblings. I have more than I ever imagined. I am blessed. You can be too but you have to let God be God in your life and obey him. I've shown you that I know the road is hard but you are on it regardless. It's just a matter of where you will end up or how? I pray blessed…

My dear sister and brother, I know this was not a conventional approach to learn about forgiveness. People are tired of being told to forgive. They are tired of being misunderstood, judged, and having their cries ignored. They are tired of pretending they trusted God because they just don't know how. They are tired of wearing a mask. Well, I took off my mask. In fact, I felt naked at times. I pray that the person needing to take this journey will bare your soul with God and get delivered. I pray the person giving advice, preaching, teaching, or ministering realizes the person they want to help isn't just angry, but they are also full of pain.

If you want to minister to others, listen to them and walk with them in love. Take them to Jesus. You may have to take this journey again with an open heart and mind and stop critiquing the message and just make it personal for them. It's time to stop wearing a mask of anger, stop hiding behind the Bible, or refusing to acknowledge that there is a God when everything around you confirms He does despite your pain. I'm sorry for your pain. Learn from it and overcome it.

It's easy to tell someone God promises to use everything for the good in their life despite their pain. I shared *My Shoes* as proof. God did show me in the end that He has a larger plan for my life, and He used everything for my good. Give Him a chance. Your story isn't over. There are pages to your life still being added. You can't change yesterday; but now, yes now, you have the power to change your today. The second part of your life doesn't have to be lived in the wilderness.

Come out. I have shared my shoes—follow God and walk out His plan for yourself.

In Loving Memory

On November 22, 2015 we had the celebration service for my dear sister Willow. My mother performed the eulogy because she said no one could convey the love of her child but her mother. And it was a home going that was unforgettable. The passing of my sister was bittersweet. She was a beautiful, talented girl who was raped as a child and never told anyone. She turned to drugs and alcohol to cope. She became filled with anger and bitterness because she didn't know how to give up the pain and get free, so she was stuck most of her life. She lived a hard, cruel life in crack houses and doing anything to support her habit. Her life was endangered many times. Willow never shared her pain or her story. I don't know who raped her; only that five years ago she told me that was why she turned to drugs. I wished I had known sooner. I wished I had known the importance of sharing our pain.

My mother prayed for her deliverance from her drugs and for her salvation. We both prayed for her heart and one day she surrendered. She gave up the drugs but it still took a little time for her to get free from the pain and anger. I don't know how it happened, but she surrendered her heart to God and love, and trust entered it again. Oh, it was a struggle—she was so mad at God. The last year I had with Willow, I was able to see my sister again. She was full of life, love, and promise.

Willow suffered with lupus' chronic pain but died of complications from congestive heart failure because of the drugs, although she had stopped using them. It was peaceful. The night before she had called all her siblings and children to share her love and encouragement. She was in a good place; always on Facebook greeting everyone with inspirationals. What a big change had come over her! Love changes everything. This woman had wanted to have nothing to do with anyone, disappearing for years at a time without any contact because the pain in her was so agonizing. But in God's grace and love, she experienced His love and surrendered. I wished we could have had more time, but her body had suffered a lot of physical abuse on the streets and God allowed her to rest.

My life experience is light in comparison to Willow's, not that we both didn't experience pain, but I didn't stay in the wilderness as long as she did. Anger was what weakened her heart. The drugs were just the vice. Love was what healed her and gave her back her life. The life on the streets she lived I couldn't have imagined or survived, but when the enemy gets in our minds and hearts we are deceived. Don't allow anger to be a stronghold over your hearts anymore; get free before it's too late. Tomorrow isn't promised. Help free the next generation; show your children how to confess their pain and forgive. Willow reconciled with all of her children, and they all honored her through testimonies, poems, and songs at the service.

So I pray all who reads this book will share it with someone else and make a commitment to stand up against abuse, secrets, and hurts. Confess your pain whatever it is, and take the journey to get to forgiveness. Learn from our *Shoes*... God bless!

About the Author

TAMMY GAFFNEY has a passion to teach and see people delivered through forgiveness. She has led life Bible groups, served in the Women's Ministry, is a lay Christian counselor and motivational speaker, and has been a registered nurse for eighteen years. She has been married to Minister Adolphus Gaffney for twenty-two years, and together they both serve at their church, New Community Bible Fellowship, in Cleveland Heights, Ohio. They have four amazing children.

Contact Information

You can email Tammy at tammygaffneysms@gmail.com and share your journey with her. You can also follow her on Facebook.